Explorations in African Biblical Studies

By

David Tuesday Adamo PhD

Wipf and Stock Publishers
150 West Broadway • Eugene OR 97401
2001

Explorations in African Biblical Studies

By Adamo, David Tuesday
Copyright©2001 by Adamo, David Tuesday
ISBN: 1-57910-682-X

Printed by *Wipf and Stock Publishers*
150 West Broadway • Eugene OR 97401

TABLE OF CONTENTS

Dedication.. ii
Acknowledgement....................................... iii
Introduction... 1

Part I African Cultural Hermeneutics at Work .. 6

African Cultural Hermeneutics......................... 7
African Background of African American Hermeneutics. 40

PART II African Biblical Studies........................... 67

Cush As Africa in the Old Testament............................ 68
Genesis Creation Account in an African Background.... 85
Deuteronomic Conception of God and Its Importance
In African Context (Deut. 6:4)..97
Peace in the Old Testament and in African Heritage... 109
Spirit (*Ruach*) in the Old Testament and in African
Context..127
Suffering in the Old Testament and in African Context.. 144
Selected Bibliography.. 164

DEDICATION

This book is dedicated to my wife, Grace Ebunlola Adamo, my sons, Oluwayomi Bamidele Adamo, David Tuesday Adamo, Jr., and my daughters Pauline Bolutife Adamo and Oluwaremilekun Adamo

ACKNOWLEDGMENTS

I am grateful to my colleague and friend, Fr. Professor Justin Ukpong, CIWA. Port Harcourt, who read this manuscript. Pauline Nolly Logan deserves the praise for reading and making corrections of the manuscript. Annelda Crawford and Barbara Bradford of St. Luke United Methodist Church, Dallas who took the pain to do the work of editing of the manuscript also deserve my thanks. I am grateful to African Baptist Church of Irving who invited me to be their pastor during my sabbatical leave. God used them to save my life.

My thanks go to my university, Delta State University, who gave a sabbatical leave and leave of absence from the university for this book is written and compiled. I am grateful to Dr. Theodore Walker, Perkins School of Theology, Southern Methodist University who did some corrections of this manuscript. Mrs Darling Yovonie deserves my gratitude for reading some of the manuscripts and did some correction.

I express my gratitude to editors of Bulletin of Biblical Studies, Bible Bhyshayam, Acton Publishers, Caribbean Journal of Religious Studies, and Sheffield Academic Press, who gave me the permission to reproduce my articles in this book.

Finally, my wife and children who endured my long absence during the writing of this book deserve so much gratitude. I am especially grateful to my beloved wife who spent so much proof reading this manuscript. That surely made it readable grammatically. Thanks to God for the miracle of life in America when I was writing this book.

David Tuesday Adamo PhD
Delta State University
Abraka, Nigeria.
June 2001

INTRODUCTION

A casual glance at the history of Hermeneutics will reveal that there has never been an interpretation that has been without references to or dependent on a particular cultural code, thought patterns, or social location of the interpreter.[1]

There is no individual who is completely detached from everything in his or her environment or experience and culture so as to be able to render one hundred percent objectiveness in everything done. The fact is that every interpreter is biased in one way or the others.[2] What I am trying to say is that there is African cultural hermeneutics because persons who are born and raised in African culture will normally interpret scriptures in ways that are unique to them and different from western interpreters. Therefore, to talk of uniform, unconditional, universal, and absolute interpretation or Hermeneutics is unrealistic. Such does not exist anywhere in this world. One who interprets tends to bring his or her own bias to bear, consciously or unconsciously, in the way in which the message is perceived.

Like the Third World biblical Hermeneutics, African biblical studies have two main characteristics: It is "liberational, and culturally sensitive." It also has some other characteristics such as narration, orality, theopoetic, and imaginative. What it does is that it uses liberation as a crucial Hermeneutics and mobilizes indigenous cultural materials for theological enterprises.[3]

Despite the Eurocentric interpreters' claims to universality, the African biblical studies are "postmodern, post colonial in its aim to celebrate the local," and

Introduction

challenge the reigning imported western theories. The African biblical studies, using African cultural hermeneutics, is hardly known and heard in western academies because such African mode of interpretation "seek to acquire and celebrate their God-given identity by delving into their indigenous resources and rejecting the superintending tendencies of western intellectual tradition."[4] This is not popular inwestern tradition not because it is incomprehensible, untranslatable to indigenous languages, but because they employ the ground rules, which differ from the normal western, rules set by the Eurocentric academy. They address issues closer home to their own people.[5] What they did was that they "learnt and borrowed ideas and techniques from external resources but reshaped them, often added their own indigenous texture, to meet their local needs."[6]

God is not a one-way track God. His mode of revelation to the world cannot be limited. God is perceived differently, depending on who you are and where you are. We are made differently. What makes sense to one person may not make sense to another. The real issue therefore is how to use our finite human knowledge and experience, and communication to speak about God who is all embracing. The fact is that no one has yet been able to invent such language to encapsulate God's completeness.[7] It looks like an impossible task, but we must keep on trying.

In African biblical studies, the Christian Bible is crucial, since this is the book or collection of books that contributes towards a disclosure about the nature of God. The fact of different translation, and versions within these translations illustrates that there are differences of interpretations as far as biblical studies and message are concerned.[8] The contention is that in Africa, some distinctive interpretations of scripture have emerged and is emerging-African cultural hermeneutics.

Most African biblical scholars are trained in the West. Those who are even trained in African higher institutions are trained and are still being trained in the Western

Introduction

tradition. After going back to Africa those of us who were trained in western tradition soon discovered that the very western methodological tradition in which we were well schooled does not satisfy the need in Africa. The result of this is to find other satisfactory ways or methodologies that will meet the need and the understanding of the African people at home and abroad. It is therefore very remarkable that African biblical scholars have tried to "forge a biblical interpretation strategy that is significantly different from that of the western interpretation."[9] This concerns relating specific biblical issues to the situation in Africa.[10] This method is different from the western methodology in that the particular focus is not only on the historical and literary context of the passage read, but also on African context. Although western critical tools and training are used, the context and the conclusion arrived at is always different from that of the western scholarship.

In these African biblical methods, there are various methods employed to achieve this purpose. These methods include are "Comparative studies, Evaluative studies, Finding African presence in the Bible, Inculturation, Liberation, Black theology, and Feminist Hermeneutics.[11] However, I concentrate on the following methods in this book: comparative, inculturation, and African presence. (1) I have used comparative methodology by comparing Old Testament and African religion and culture (2) I have also briefly exposed the presence of Africa and Africans in the Old Testament.[12] (3) I have employed inculturation and liberation Hermeneutics for this research. These methodologies are used in conjunction with western methodologies.

African biblical scholarship, using what I also called African cultural hermeneutics as its methodology, is at its infancy. I hope that African biblical scholars will continue to forge ahead to achieve significant progress in this matter.

What I have been trying to say is that African biblical studies still owe much to both western and African tradition. It does not reject one approach to the total

Introduction

exclusion of the other. It affirms that there is something to gain in all human Hermeneutics. African cultural hermeneutics can learn from different methods, including historical-critical, allegorical, form and other methodologies.

This book is a collection of some of my articles since the beginning of my teaching career in many universities in the United States and Africa. Some of these essays have been published and reworked. Others have not been published. They contain my experience and my attempt to make biblical studies relevant to African Christianity. In the process of reading this book, it is important for the readers to relax their ideas and misconceptions about Africa and Africans so that new ideas about African Christianity, no matter how strange and radical it might be, may receive an objective consideration. This is important since every idea is perspectival.

Endnotes

[1] George Mulrain, "*Hermeneutics* within a Caribbean Context," *Vernacular Hermeneutics*, ed. R.S Sugirtharajah (Sheffeild: Sheffield Academy Press, 1999), 116-132.
[2] Ibid.
[3] R.S.Sugirtharajah, "Vernacular Resurrections: An Introduction," *Vernacular Hermeneutics*, (ed.) R.S Sugirtharajah,, 11.
[4] Ibid.
[5] Ibid., 12-13.
[6] Ibid. "Thinking about Vernacular Hermeneutics Sitting in a Metropolitan Study," *Vernacular Hemeneutics*, 108
[7] George Mulrain, "Hermeneutics within a Caribbean Context, *Vernacular Hermeneutics*, 117-121.
[8] Ibid.
[9] Justin S. Ukpong, "Can African Old Testament Scholarship escape the historical critical approach?" *Newsletter on African Old Testament Scholarship*, Knut Holter (ed.), no 7, (1999), 2.
[10] Ibid.
[11] Ibid. 3
[12] David Tuesday Adamo, *Africa and the Africans in the Old Testament* (San Francisco: Christian Universities Press, 1998). Detail study of the presence of Africa and the Africans is done in this book. This book is reprinter by the Wipf and Stock Publishers, Eugene, Oregon. My readers should examine this book if they are interested in more information about the presence of Africa and Africans in the Old Testament.

PART I

AFRICAN BIBLICAL HERMENEUTICS AT WORK

African Cultural Hermeneutics[1]

Introduction

In African indigenous culture, the means of dealing successfully with traditional problems like diseases, sorcerers, witches, enemies, and lack of success in life experiences, have been developed. Western miss ionaries taught African Christians to discard these indigenous ways of handling these problems without offering any concrete substitute, except the Bible. Charms, medicine, incantations, divination, sacrifices and other cultural ways of protecting, healing and liberating ourselves from the evil powers that fill African forests were hurriedly discarded in the name of Christianity. Yet, we were not taught how to use that Bible as a means of protecting, healing, and solving the daily problems of life. The Euro-American way of reading the Bible has not actually helped us to understand the Bible in our own context.[2]

Faced with some peculiar problems as African Christians, we search the Bible consistently with our own eyes in order to discover whether there could be anything in the Bible that can solve our problems. In the process of reading the Bible in our own eyes, we discovered in the scripture great affinities with our own worldview and culture. We discovered in both the Old and New Testaments resemblance to events similar to the African experience, especially painful experiences. Examples of these activities are miracles, encounter with satanic powers, the reality of hunger and the deliverance of the oppressed. In the miracles that were narrated in the Bible, many means of healing were used-medicine, the mere pronouncement of words, touching, prayers, and ordinary water. We then started asking questions as to how to read the Bible with our own eyes to meet our daily needs as African Christians. The attempt to answer these questions brought about the introduction of African cultural hermeneutics or vernacular Hermeneutics.

This book section shows how indigenous churches employ African cultural hermeneutics to interpret the Bible in African context. This essay will illustrate in the most concrete way in which African Indigenous Churches have applied the African cultural hermeneutics to the Bible, especially Psalms. This is one of the sections where my readers need to relax their old ideas and prejudices about Africa for the purpose of objectivity.

Definition of African cultural hermeneutics

African cultural hermeneutics in biblical studies is an approach to biblical interpretation that makes African social cultural context a subject of interpretation.[3] It means that African cultural hermeneutics, like any other Third World Hermeneutics, is contextual Hermeneutics since interpretation is always done in a particular context. Specifically it means that analysis of the text is done from the perspective of African world-view and culture.⁴ African cultural hermeneutics is rereading the scripture from a premeditatedly Africentric perspective. The purpose is not only to understand the Bible and God in our African experience and culture, but to breaking the Hermeneutical hegemony and ideological stranglehold that Eurocentric biblical scholars have long enjoyed.⁵ This is a methodology that reappraises ancient biblical tradition and African world-view, culture, and life experience with the purpose of "correcting the effect of the cultural ideological conditioning to which Africa and Africans have been subjected." Several terms appear synonymous to this African cultural hermeneutics: inculturation Hermeneutics,⁶ liberation hermeneutics,⁷ contextual hermeneutics,⁸ Africentric hermeneutics,⁹ and vernacular hermeneutics.¹⁰ I will not spend much time defining African cultural hermeneutics. Rather, I will demonstrate the way this type of Hermeneutics is used in Africa, especially Nigeria.

Conditions for African cultural Hermeneutics

In order to do African cultural hermeneutics successfully, some conditions are important and should be mentioned as guide:

1. The interpreter must be an insider. This means that the would-be interpreter must be either an African or live and experience all aspects of African life in Africa. By this it is difficult to do African cultural hermeneutics without living in Africa and going through, the joy, problems of poverty, ethnicity, hunger, communalism and other palatable and unpalatable aspects of African culture.

2.He or she must be immersed in the content of the Bible It is not enough just to know the content, it is absolutely necessary to believe the stories and the event of the Bible as a life of faith. In other words, the biblical events are reflections of our own present individual and communal life. The interpreter must be a person of faith. There must be a firm belief in the power of God's word.

3. Understanding African indigenous culture is absolutely important in doing African cultural hermeneutics. This is because African culture is part and parcel of African cultural hermeneutics. Despite the resemblance of the biblical and African cultures, there are still some distinct aspects of African culture. These distinctive African culture influences or dominates the interpretation of the Bible.

4. Faith in God who is all powerful is important condition for African Cultural Hermeneutics. This fiath in God is not only in His existence but also in His absolute power to perform miracle. Faith in Him that He is in control of all things in heaven and on earth. He can heal, protect, and grant success in life.

5. Ability to read or memorize the words of the Bible is important. The interpreter may not necessarily be a scholar of the Bible. Some of the evangelists in Africa are illiterate, yet they use the word of God to perform miracles and wonders in Africa. Some blind evangelists have good memories to memorize the Bible. They have also used the words of God to achieve great things in Africa.

The above conditions will be reflected in the example of interpretation of Psalms below:

The Importance of the Book of Psalms

I choose the book of Psalms because of its important place among the Old Testament books of the Bible. This is why the book of Isaiah and Psalms are the most frequently quoted books of the Old Testament in the New Testament. This is the book of the Bible that the Christian community found the easiest to approach personally and directly in the time of joy, sorrow, pain, confusion and danger.[11] B.W Anderson was emphatic on the unique place given to the book of Psalms by the Christian Church. Faith in God who is all-powerful is an important condition for African cultural hermeneutics. This faith in God is not only in his existence but also in his absolute power to do and undo. He is in control and he performs miracles at will. This God can use any means to heal, protect, and bring success in all life endeavor.

> Today in Roman Catholic and Eastern Orthodox Churches especially where the ancient monastic usage is still preserved the entire Psalter is recited once each week. In the Anglican (church) the Psalter are repeated once a month. And in other churches in the Protestant tradition the profound influence of the Psalter is evident in responsive reading of selected Psalms or in the singing of hymns. Indeed, when one considers the enriching and invigorating influence which the Psalms have exerted on preaching, worship and devotional life, it is no exaggeration for Christopjh Barth to say that the renewal and reunion of the church, for which we are hoping, cannot come about without the powerful assistance of Psalms.[12]

The writers of Christian hymns throughout centuries have drawn from the well of Psalter. Apart from its use in public worship, individuals have found edification and comfort in sorrow and afflictions in the book of Psalms. The Psalter speaks about God and to God in such a way that no other book has done. That is why it is the favorite book of all the saints.[13] Quoting Martin Luther, Weiser writes,

> To sum up: if you want to see the holy Christian Church painted in glowing colours and in a form which is really alive, and if you want this to be done in a miniature, you must get hold of the Psalter, and there you will have in your possession a fine, clear, pure mirror which will show you what Christianity really is; yea, you will find yourself in it and the true *'gnothi seauton'* ('know thyself) God himself and all his creatures, too.[14]

The book of Psalms is important among the books of the Bible. That is why throughout the Christian centuries, the Psalms have received special attention among Christians all over the world. This unique place of Psalms in the

Christian Churches has influenced biblical scholars to struggle continuously to discover the correct approaches for understanding the book of Psalms. The Western scholars are champions of this struggle. These approaches include, determining the authors and dates of Psalms according to the superscription, determining the literary types and forms, and the basic theological thought of the Psalms.

However, to many Africans who were converted to Christianity, the above approaches by Western scholars appear too mechanical. Such approaches do not meet the daily needs of the Africans who are confronted with what to eat, how to diffuse the power of enemies, diseases, and even death. Africans who were given the Bible and faith in God as substitutes, constantly faced the questions, how do we use faith and the Bible as concrete and effective substitutes for our traditional way of protection, healing and success, that is, as protection against enemies, and evil spirits, to heal sicknesses and to bring successes at work, in schools and in businesses? The answer to these questions have been found by the African Indigenous Churches who have used the African cultural hermeneutics to discover the distinctive ways of classifying the Psalms into Protective, curative or therapeutic, and success Psalms and use them in conjunction with other natural materials.

Protective Use of Psalms.

Protection in African Indigenous Culture.

It is important to discuss protection in African indigenous culture before going on to the use of protective Psalms. The existence of evil ones is painfully real in African indigenous tradition. Witches, sorcerers, wizards, evil spirits and all ill-wishers are considered enemies. The consciousness of these enemies is a major source of fear and anxiety in African indigenous society. Among the Yoruba people of

Nigeria, there is a belief that every person has at least, one known or unknown enemy called *ota*. The activities of *ota* can bring painful consequences. It may be abnormal behavior, sudden loss of children and property, chronic illness and even death. To express how powerful and wicked the activities of witches who are also enemies of the society, Primate J.O .S Ayelabola narrated the confession of a witch:

> We drink human blood in the day or night....
> We can prevent a sore from healing;
> We can make a person to loose a large sum of money;
> We can reduce a great man to nothing;
> We can send a small child to heaven suddenly;
> We can cause a woman to bear born-to-die children (*abiku*).[15]

The belief in enemies as the main sources of all evil and bad occurrences is so strong that nothing happens naturally without a spiritual force behind it. Thus incidents like infant mortality, bareness in women, impotence in men, accident of any kind, dullness in school children and all other bad things are attributed to enemies of different kinds. Constant fear and insecurity may also be caused by hostile environment other than malignant forces. Events such as road and fire accidents, gunshot and cutlass injuries can also be caused by hostile environment. People therefore do go to medicine person to prevent or protect themselves from such attacks.

Before the advent of Christianity, Africans had a cultural way of dealing with the problem of enemies and all evil ones. There are various techniques of making use of natural materials and potent powerful words that they put to defensive and offensive use in dealing with evil ones. One of the cultural ways of protection against enemies is the use of imprecatory spoken words (the so-called incantations) called *ogede* in Yoruba language. Traditionally when an African identifies an enemy and does not have the potent words or medicine to deal with such enemy, such a person consults a medicine man *(babalawo* or *onisegun* or *oologun* in Yoruba language) who prepares or teaches the person some potent words or give a charm for protection or for attacking the enemy. A perfect example of the type of potent words used among the Yoruba society to make a sorcerer lose his or her senses is stated below:

> *Igbagbe se oro ko lewe (3times)*
> *Igbagbe se afomo ko legbo (3 times)*
> *Igbagbe se Olodumare ko ranti la ese pepeye (3 times)*
> *Nijo ti pepeye ba daran egba igbe hoho ni Ki igbagbe se lagbaja omo lagbaja ko maa wogbo lo*
> *Tori t 'odo ba nsan ki iwo ehin moo*

Translation

> Due to forgetfulness the oro (cactus) plant has no leaves (3 times)
> Due to forgetfulness the *Afomo* (misletoes) plant has no roots (3 times)
> Due to forgetfulness god did not remember to separate the toes of the duck (3 times)
> When the duck is beaten it cries, hoho
> May forgetfulness come upon (name the enemy), the son/daughter of (name the mother);
> that is, may he loose his senses.
> That he or she may enter into the bush
> Because a flowing river does not flow backward and so on.

The above potent words can be repeated two or three times or more without any addition.
Another major way of obtaining protection against enemies mentioned above in African societies is the use of charms or amulets. The medicine men and women who are healers and diviners usually prepare amulets and charms for those who need it. They are used for diverse purposes but mainly as protective devices to prevent enemies, witches and wizard, and evil spirits from entering a house and attacking a person. It is also used to nullify all the

attempts of enemies or sorcerers. They contain different ingredients according to the purpose of the charm or amulets. For example, a charm for the purpose of hanging on the doorframe for protection are made of "seven leaves of some plants, and seven seeds of alligator pepper." Charms to be tied around one's neck for protection against enemies may require alligator peppers, white and red cola-nuts and the blood of a cock. Charms are wrapped with animal skin and sewn round. Others are wrapped inside pieces of cloth or paper and tied with some black and white threads. Some also require the recitation of some potent words and prayer to accompany the charms for the purpose of effectiveness.[16] Those words must be recited exactly according to the prescription of the medicine-man otherwise it may not be efficacious. A person can obtain charms for the purpose of protection against motor accident and crash. In traditional Africa, hunters who hunt in the bush at night will normally protect themselves with charms against wild animal attack, snakebites, and against wicked supernatural beings such as *iwin* and *aunjonu*. A person may also obtain charms for the purpose of protection against motor accident and air crash on a journey.

Identification of Protective Psalms in African Indigenous Churches

African converts to Christianity were forbidden to practice African cultural ways of protection because they were labeled as paganistic and abominable to God. Unfortunately the Yoruba concerns with protection, healing, and success are not adequately addressed by the Eurocentric version of Christianity. At a point among the Yoruba people of Nigerian, men who accepted this type of Christianity without arming themselves with African power of Words, amulets, and charms were ridiculed and called women. To the Yoruba non-Christians, Christianity was an impotent religion. More unfortunate was the fact that Western Christianity that was introduced to Africans did not reveal the secrets of western power and knowledge, but instead revealed prejudice and oppression in the missionary support for colonial masters. The type of Christianity introduced to African Christian did not meet the present need of the Africans-protection, healing and success. They started to suspect that there must be more to Christianity that missionaries did not reveal to them. African Indigenous Christians sought vigorously for that hidden treasures in the missionary religion that was hidden from them. They sought it in the Bible in their own way and in their own culture. Using African cultural hermeneutics to interpret the Bible, they found that there are secret powers in the Bible, especially in the book of Psalms. They use the Bible protectively, therapeutically, and successfully to fill the missing gap left by the Eurocentric Christianity. As African Christians search the Bible to find potent words for protection against perennial problem of witches and all forces of evil, they suddenly discovered some words in the book of Psalms that resemble the ones used in African tradition against enemies. They discovered that the words of these Psalms are not only potent they lend themselves to imprecatory use like that of African tradition. They classified Psalms 5, 6, 28, 35, 37, 54, 55, 83, 109 as protective Psalms. Some of them are imprecatory by contents. Most of these Psalms belong to the classification of the individual and community lament. It reflects the individual and the community cry to God with lament and confession and trust, petition and the promise of praise.[17]

The following are Psalms that contain curses on the enemies of the Psalmist and rejoicing over the enemies' downfall:

> Make them bear their guilt O God;
> Let them fall by their own counsels,
> because of their many transgressions
> ....All my enemies shall be shamed
> and sorely troubled; they shall turn

African Cultural Hermeneutics

back and be put to shame in a moment(RSV. 5.10).

Sometimes the Psalmists invoke death to come upon their enemies. Psalm 55:15, 23 says:

> Let death come upon them;
> Let them go down to Sheol alive;
> Let them go away in terror into their grave....
> (they) shall not live out half their days (RSV).

They regarded this Psalm as Psalm for protection against enemies since it makes them "die by their own evil deeds."[18] This Psalm should be read everyday. The holy name of God *Jah* should also be pronounced after each reading of the Psalm. The belief in God's saving grace is important as one reads this Psalm. It will protect a person against the plan of enemies. They will perish by their own evil deeds. Chief J Ogunfuye prescribes Psalm 109 for use against enemies. According to him one will need to go to an open field in the middle of a night or 1.PM. Three candles should be lighted, one in the North, one in the East, and one in the West, while standing in the middle. Read the Psalm with the name of *El*, the name of the enemy and that of his or her mother in mind. Pray the following prayer:

> Almighty God (name your enemy),
> the son or daughter of (name his or her mother)
> is after me to destroy me.
> Oh Lord of hosts,
> I beseech in thy mercy....
> Let his or her wicked deeds come back to him/her
> And let him/her perish in his/her evil designs
> Put him/her to shame....[19]

In African context, Psalm 35 is used to drive away evil plans of enemies and especially witches and evil men. Read this Psalm in conjunction with prayers between midnight and three O'clock in the night in the open air while the reader is naked. As in Yoruba tradition Psalms are also made into amulets to be worn around the neck or around

African Cultural Hermeneutics

the body. Chief J.O Ogunfuye specializes in the preparation of Psalms into amulets for different usage. For protection against enemies and the evil one, he prescribes Psalm 7. According to him, there are two ways to prepare this Psalm for defending oneself against secret enemies or evil forces that planned to ruin a person. A person should read this Psalm with the holy name *Eel Elikon* with a special prayer every day. Below is the prayer to accompany this Psalm:

> O merciful Father, Almighty and everlasting King,
> I beseech Thee in the holy name of *Eel Elijon* to deliver
> me from all secret enemies and evil spirits
> that plan my destruction always.
> Protect me from their onslaught and let their evil forces
> be turned back upon them
> Let their expectation come to nought and let them fail
> in their bid to injure me.
> Let their ways be dark and slippery and let thy holy angels disperse them so that they may not come high unto my dwelling place. Hear my prayer now for the sake of holy Eel Elijon.[20]

Some prophets of the indigenous churches prescribe some Psalms for prevention of flood catastrophes, fire disasters, protection of soldiers in the battlefield, police officers, and hunters. Psalm 60 is one of the Psalms prescribed for such people and should be read with the name *Jah*.[21]

Therapeutic Use of Psalms in African Indigenous Churches

Before the advent of Christianity and western medicine, Africans have developed certain effective ways of rescuing themselves from these types of diseases. These ways include the use of herbs, powerful, mysterious or potent words animal parts, living and non-living things, water, fasting, praying, laying of hands, and other rituals for restoration of harmony among people and the environment.

Massaging as a therapeutic system is another important system of healing which is effective for the treatment of nervous, muscular systems and especially that of gynecological problems.[22] Hydro-therapy is another means by which Africans rescue themselves from pain and other ailments. Hydro-therapy involves the use of cold, or hot water. Compress and steam vapor baths can be used for different diseases like headache, fever, rheumatism and general pains. Hot water relaxes the skin capillaries and the activity of the sweat glands.[23] Water increases the consumption of oxygen up to about 75% and it eliminates about 85% of carbon dioxide in the body.[24] Fasting is an important aspect of indigenous therapeutic methods in Africa. To cure an ailment, patients are instructed to abstain from food ofr cetain period of days or weeks. This method is usually used to cure obesity, indigestion, Fasting is an important aspect of indigenous therapeutic methods in Africa. To cure an ailment, patients are instructed to abstain from food for a period of days or weeks. This method is usually used for curing obesity, indigestion, overweight, mental and some chronic diseases. Mume is very sure of the good result of fasting in curing diseases. He says that fasting is

> the most effective means of body house cleaning known. Fasting is an eliminator of accumulated toxins as well as a general restorative. Fasting is a purifying process. It brings about a rapid elimination of toxic elements and poisonous materials from the body.[25]

Another important method of healing is what we may call faith-healing method. In African Indigenous Religion, especially in ancestor worship, a person who is tortured by the ancestors is asked to confess and make sacrifices.
After all these have been done, the offender is made to believe that he has been forgiven and healed of the

sickness.

The use of potent words, for therapeutic purposes is not uncommon among African indigenous people. These words have to be spoken in a specific place, at specific time and in a specific way for them to be effective.

There are medicines for various illnesses, such as snake bite, scorpion sting, and difficult delivery for pregnant women, and dull memory for students. After chewing seven alligator peppers, and placing one's mouth on the patient's navel one should recite the potent words below to cure scorpion sting and headache:

Oorun lode l'alamu wonu,
Oorun kuju alaamu jade(7 times)

Translation:

When the sun is hot the female lizard
appears (7 times).
When the sun softens, the female lizard appears.[26]

A woman who has a history of miscarriages or infant mortality should immediately start using a concoction fo a pregnant woman call *agbo aboyun*. Likewise a woman who has become aware that she is pregnant should begin with the same concoction. Important potent words for a pregnant woman for a safe delivery are:

Kankan l'ewe ina njomo
Kan kan ni ki lagbaja omo lagbaja
bi mo re loni
Konu koho ki roju ti fifi aso re toro
Ki lagbaja omo lagbaja a ma
roju ti ofi bi omo re loni.

Translation

The leave of *ina* burns in haste
(name the labouring woman)
the daughter of (name her mother)
should deliver her child in haste today

African Cultural Hermeneutics

The *Konu koho* tree does not hesitate
to give off its cloth bark (name the labouring woman)
The daughter of (name the mother)
should not hesitate to deliver her child today
Because the snake sheds it skin easily.[27]

Identification of Therapeutic Psalms

As stated above, when western missionaries came to West Africa, they concluded that indigenous therapeutic methods were barbaric, and even abominable. With the total devotion of missionaries who left their beautiful countries to the African jungle, and with the emphasis on the importance of the Christian book, there must be something equally potent that could be used for healing. The discovery of Psalm as equally potent as the indigenous words for healing aroused great interest in the book of Psalms. Some Psalms are therefore, classified as therapeutic Psalms. The readings of such Psalms are combined with African indigenous method of healing. Absolute faith in the word of God and in God himself is maintained but with the combination of herbs, prayer, fasting, and the use of the name of God in the healing process. Members of African Indigenous Churches believed that virtually all types of illnesses are curable with the combination of reading Psalms and the use of materials.

According to T.N.Adeboyejo, Psalm 1, 2, and 3 are special Psalms for stomach pain, and for these Psalms to be effective one should mix fried oil, potash, small salt and egg into water. Then Psalms 1, 2, 3 should be read into it for drinking little by little. According to Adeboyejo, the patient will surely be healed.[28]

For swollen stomach, he recommends Psalms 20 and 40. One should get water from a flowing river into a new pot. Put together a complete palm front and three new grown up Palm leaf in the pot. While reading Psalm 20 and 40 with the holy name *ELI SAFATAN* (62 times), one should light nine candles. The reader should bathe with the water for nine days.[29] Or one could read these Psalms into mixed fried oil, coconut oil, some cow urine and cheer oil. The

Holy name above could be read over it for drinking and bathing and rubbing over the body.[30] Bolarinwa believes that these Psalms are potent to cure toothache, headache and backache. For toothache, these psalms could be read into a lukewarm water and use to rinse mouth with until the tumbler is empty.[31] The process can be repeated from time to time.

For barren women to have children, Psalms 51, Gen. 15.1-5, 21.1-8, I Sam. 1.9-20 should be read three times into coconut water or raw native egg with prayer and drunk.[32] The action above should be done very early in the morning and nakedly after a woman might have known her husband. The following names should be called for effectiveness: *Jehovah Shiklo-hirami* (21 times) *and Holy Mary (*12 times).

Chief Oguntuye recognizes Psalm 6 as the one to relieve a sick person of pains and worries. It is also good for stomach trouble, eye trouble or any ailment. The sick person should read the Psalm in great humility and with special prayer and the mentioning of the holy names *Jaschaja; Bali; Hashina* in mind. According to him all her worries will be removed. Below is the special prayer to be offered to accompany this Psalm for effective healing:

> O Lord God and Prince of Peace, I beseech Thee in the name of *Jaschaja, Bali, Hashina* to hear me and speedily heal me from this diseases that troubles me (name the diseases). Wipe away my tears and turn my sorrow into joy. Give unto me Thy wonderful grace to overcome all manner of diseases. Restore unto me my former health
> and silent all my adversaries for ever. Forgive me all my sins and sustain me with Thy grace all the days of my life.
> Pour thy blessings upon me from above and let my prayers be acceptable in Thy sight so that I may glorify thy holy name forever. Amen.[33]

If the patient does not know how to read, someone should read for him or her but his or her name and the name of his or her mother must be mentioned.

One of the major problems in Africa is bareness and infant mortality. This is mostly responsible for family break up and polygamy. In most indigenous societies in Africa, as priests and diviners are contacted before any marriage contract to make sure that the spouse will not be barren or face infant mortality, so also have some therapeutic Psalms been identified as effective cure for such problems.

Psalm 1 that compares the way of the wicked with the righteous is used therapeutically to cure gynecological problems such as miscarriages in women. When a woman is aware that she is pregnant, she should read Psalm 1 daily in the morning and evening. The process should be accompanied by prayer in the name of *Eli-Ishaddi, Jehovah shallom*.[34] Psalms 126 that are prayers to God to restore Israelite fortunes is said to be efficacious for infant mortality.[35] A woman with a history of past experiences of infant mortality should start reading this Psalm immediately after she is aware of her pregnancy. This Psalm should be read into water for bathing washing and drinking daily throughout the period of her pregnancy. The same process should also continue immediately after delivery to wash the baby until it is fully grown. With the reading of this Psalms as instructed, early death of such child is unthinkable. Psalm 126 could also be written on four pure parchments with the holy names *Sinni, Sinsuni and Semanflaf*. This parchment should be kept in the four corners of a house whenever pregnancy occurs by a person with the history of giving birth to born-to-die children (*abiku* in Yoruba and *ogbanje* in Ibo of Nigeria). Psalm 16 is recommended for safe and easy delivery. It is to be read three times over water by a pregnant woman for drinking and bathing with holy name JEHOVAH JARRABBILLAH (three times).[36]

These therapeutic Psalms are many and are also prescribed according to the type of illness. Psalms for fearfulness (127), chronic diseases (21), too long term pregnancy (27,28,29, 16), epilepsy (100, 109, 102) are examples of these Psalms. It is certain that these methods of reading Psalms therapeutically are dictated by African cultural influence on African indigenous Christians. The search for classifying the entire Bible to meet the daily need of African indigenous Christians is still on not only because modern medicine is not available or may never be available to all in Africa, but also because indigenous medicine is effective and Christian.

Indigenous System for Securing Success

The examination of the classification of some Psalms into successful Psalms will be more understood and intelligible with the discussion of the use of medicine and potent words to enhance success in all walks of life in African indigenous tradition.

Success in all walks of life is an important aspect of Nigerian Society. Lack of success is viewed with all seriousness. Success in academic life (especially passing exams), business, a journey, securing love from a person, and success over court cases are sought after. African indigenous medicine for activating or improving memory abounds. Such medicine, among the Yoruba people of Nigeria, is called *isoye*. Isoye in Yoruba practically means "quickening the memory or intelligence."[37] It refers to any medicine that can help to quicken memory. Below is an example of such medicine prescribed by a traditional healer to one of my former students for success in examination:

> A combination of honey, *eeran* leaves, *awerepepe* leaves and one Alligator pepper.
> All should be burnt together and mixed with honey.
> The client licks from the concoction and spits it into his left palm.

There is a firm assurance that the client will be successful in the examination. Another important way by which African indigenous people try to bring success to themselves is the use of medicine called *awure* in Yoruba. It literally means the thing that activates success or what uncovers success. This type of medicine that brings good luck may be in the form of potent words, soap, or a mixture of herbs and other ingredients to make a concoction. Whenever an important venture is being embarked upon, in African indigenous tradition, a strong awareness that enemies (man or spirits, seen and unseen), who are struggling to bring bad luck to people abound despite all ability to succeed. This thought is indisputable in a typical African traditional society. Hence, when an important venture like business, building houses, marriage, hunting for a new job, or attending an interview, a medicine-man is often consulted to narrow down the chances of failure and increase success.

Identification of Success Psalms

The Psalms that are identified as success Psalms are those believed by the African Indigenous Churches to have the power to bring success if used with faith, and rituals, such as prayer, fasting, and rehearsal of some specific symbols, and a combination of other animate or inanimate materials. Christians in Africa who were not comfortable in using pure indigenous ways of obtaining success mostly because of the condemnation by the western orthodox Christians and missionaries, had no choice but to find the alternative method of achieving success. They turned to the Christian Bible, and found, in the book Psalms, the equivalent powers, that they had discarded.

Success in Examination

For success in examination or studies, Psalms 4,8.1-9,9,23,24,27,46,51,119.9-16,134 are identified. For students who want to improve their memory and be sure of success in all their examination Psalms 4 should be used with this instruction:

> cut four candles into three each,
> light them round and be in the middle of the candles,
> put some salts under each candle, read Psalm 4 (8 times).
> Call Holy Name *ALATULA JAH AJARAHLIAH* (72 times).
> Pray for success. You will surely pass.[38]

Psalm 8.1-9 is also recommended for success in

examination.[39] The name of the school where the examination is to be taken should be written in a parchment paper. At the bottom of the paper write the following holy names: *Jah-Jubrillah, Elli-Apejubba, Elli-Majjubbah, Elli-Jah-bubbih, Elli-- 11ah* (mention the name of the person who is taking the examination and the name of the place where the examination is taking place). Mention also *Jehovah Ellisaittah* three times (Amen) Sellah. Burn the paper to ashes, divide it into two, one inside water for drinking before going to examination and the remaining should be put in Olive oil or *bintu* (perfume) for anointing oneself. It is sure that the person writing the examination will pass.

In order to sharpen one's memory, Psalms 9, 24, 27, and 46 are recommended by the Prophet Sam Akin Adewole with specific instructions to be followed.[40]

> 7 coconut water should be used to boil 3 native eggs. The water should be kept safely in a bowl and the eggs in another white dish put honey (a bottle) close to the materials. Light seven candles round the children, preferably in the Mercy Land or Church in your prayer room. Burn heavy incense and sprinkle original perfume. Sing 3 songs for the forgiveness 3 for mercy and the last for thanks. Call the following Holy names: Jah-Jehova 7 times Jesus Christ " Holy Mother Mary (7 times)
> Jehova Shico Hiramy(7times)
> Jehovah Ellion (7 times)
> Jehova Jireh "(7 times)
> El-braka-bred-El (7 times)
> Psalms 51, 27, 24, 9, 46, Isa 60, II Chron. 9.13-28 should be read.

The whole ritual should start on Tuesday night till Thursday night. If there are many children in the house use 3 eggs for each of them for three days after the work. With a candle in their hands, use the candle to pray for them after each vigil. This should be repeated monthly with the prophet's loin or girdle to wipe their heads and pray for them. With this the students will be successful. In another booklet the Prophet Adewole prescribes Psalms 23 and 51 (to be read in conjunction with I Kgs. 3.1-14)[41] for students as *Isoye* (medicine to sharpen one's memory) for them to be successful in examination.

T.N Adeboyejo also prescribes Psalms 119.9-16 for sharp memory. According to him, one native egg should be cooked well, remove its shell and put it in a cup or glass of water and read Psalm 119.9-16 into it in conjunction with Deut. 33.1-3, Joshua1.1-8 and eat the egg once. However, one may choose to read the word of God over honey or olive oil to lick or drink.

For success to love a woman or man

Psalm 133 is a Psalm classified as the one that will aid one to secure love of a person. For example if any man is looking for a girl friend or a lovely wife and had a history of failure in such endeavor, if a woman is looking for a boyfriend or a husband; if a wife is loosing the love of her husband; if a husband is looking for the love of his spouse who may be on the verge of divorce, he or she should read this Psalm with the following important instruction.

> Draw some water with your mouth into a bottle. Put some water that will fill the bottle into a bowl. Wash your face and armpits seven times in the water in the bow. Add that water in the bow to the one in the bottle to fill it up. Then call the name of the woman or man and the name Eve or Adam (21 times). Read Psalms 133, Ruth 1.16-17 and Song of Solomon 3:1-11 and John 1.1-4 into the water at midnight and if the person is known, give the water to her/him to drink.[42]

Chief Oguntuye recommends this Psalm 133 for husband and wife, family, society or church to avoid disharmony.[43]

Success in Court Cases

For success or good luck in winning court cases Psalms 13, 35, 46, 51, 77, 83, 87, 91, 110, 121, and 148 with specific instructions are recommended. Whenever it is three days to go to court for a specific case, fast for three days and after that stand in the midst of the congregation with a sincere confession of sins silently. Let all the congregation prays for you. Before the case starts, take one coconut, three candles and a big stone. Light the candles before starting. Break the coconut on a big stone. Read Psalms 13, 51, 77, 83, 110 seven times. Read also Psalms 35 and 148 three times. Call the names Holy Michael to the East, Holy Gabriel to the West, Holy Raphael to the North, and Holy Uriel Roller to the South. With the Holy Name *Jehovah-Aturakaja* seven times. Say the case of (your name) and (the other person's name) become... *WOMWOMWOB* seven times. Let me win. While holding the coconut, say that the day that any coconut knocks the stone it will break into pieces. Then knock the coconut very hard on that stone by force and say IN THE NAME OF JESUS CHRIST while knocking the coconut on the stone.[44]

Success in Business

Psalm 4, 108, and 114 are special Psalms for success in any venture one embarks on such as laying the foundation of a house, promotion in government work, embarking on a business trip. These Psalms are to be read with prescribed instruction and prayers to accompany them. Chief Ogunfuye recommends Psalm 4 for success in any business or in any undertaking. This Psalm has to be read with the holy name *Jehovah Sella Jiheje* including the prayers below seven times with faith every morning before sunrise. Below is the Prayer to accompany the above Psalm:

> Almighty God and holy *Jiheje*, I commend unto Thee my work and all my desires. I beseech Thee in Thy great holy name to prosper my work and give me victory over all my adversaries. Crown all my efforts with success and lead me in the paths of righteousness always. Hear my prayer this morning for the sake of Thy adorable holy name *Jehovah Sella Jiheje*. Amen.[45]

African Cultural Hermeneutics

Ogunfuye also recommends Psalm 114 for success in business of any kind. It should be read from time to time in the morning with the name of *Aha* and *Adonai* in mind. Below is the special prayer to accompany this Psalm:

> My Father and my King, I humbly beseech Thee to give me Thy grace and bless me receive the help and good-will of all people so that my work may continue to grow bigger and stronger. Direct unto me good and reliable customers and give me Thy heavenly wisdom to direct my business according to Thy Holy will. Give me sound health and enough energy to run my daily race with success. Hear my prayer and let my supplications come before Thy throne for the sake of Thy throne for the sake of Thy holy name. Amen.[46]

There are Psalms that are regarded as useful for general success and progress of all kinds. Examples of such Psalms are Psalms 1 and 67. Psalm 1 is to be read very often with the holy name *Eel Chad, Jehovah Shalom*. It is to be read in conjunction with some specific prayers and trust in the all-saving grace of the Almighty God. Such a person will always be successful in all his ways and whatever he sets his or her hands on will be fruitful.

Psalm 67 is to be read always with the holy name *Hah, Jekonenu Jehumu,* and then have belief in almighty God who is the fountain of all goodness. General success and progress is sure to come to the person.[47] Every Psalm is assigned for special purpose either to cure, for special types of sickness, for success, or for general or special type of protection.

Critical Evaluation of the Use of Psalms in African Indigenous Churches

The Division of Psalms

The division of Psalms into types in African indigenous churches is informed mostly by the contents of the Psalms as understood by African Christian-laymen, prophets,

African Cultural Hermeneutics

pastors and evangelists. Some of the Psalms that are called Protective Psalms belong to what scholars of form criticism call the individual and community lament. The content of these Psalms are mainly the cry of God's people and their wish for their prayers to be answered by eliminating the enemies.[48] The therapeutic Psalms are Psalms which belong to the western classification of the combination of Individual and communal Lament, thanksgiving, Wisdom Hymn and Praise of God. Success Psalms include all kinds of western classification of Psalms such Psalms of praise, lament, and wisdom.

The Use of Names

A close examination of the use of Psalms in African Indigenous Churches above shows that the use of names is predominant. Some of the names that are recited or invoked are names of God such as *Yahweh, Elohim, Adonai,* names of angels such as Gabriel, Michael, Uriel, and some unknown names such as *Alatulah, Ja, Ajarahlial, Ehala, Selidira, Tabbih, Jaschaja, Bali, Hashina Walola, Asabata Ja,* and *womwomwoba.* During my visit to some of these indigenous churches, I found out that some of the names used are names of God that describe his activities such as *Jehovah Jireh,*[49] *Jehovah Nissi, Jehovah Shallom, Jehovah Shammah, Jehovah Tsidkenu,*[50] *Jehovah Rophe,*[51] *El Shaddai*[52]*, Hehovah Mkeddesh, Jehovah Rohi*[53]*, Jehovah Shaphat,*[54] *Jehovah Zadak*[55]*, Jehovah Zabad, Jehovah Emmanuel.*[56] In addition, names of enemies, judges, mothers, women, and names of persons are generally mentioned. Although some of these names are Hebrew names from the Old Testament, they are not properly spelt or pronounced. This is probably because the users are not literate in biblical Hebrew. However, during my interview with some of the prophets and apostles of these churches, they claimed that these names were revealed. The truth is that some of these names are unbiblical and unknown to me and many other scholars and pastors of the mainline missionary churches in Africa. Despite the fact that some of these names are not known, the invocation of names in the use of Psalms is quite in line with African culture, but as well as with the Bible.[57]

Among Africans, names are not only symbolic, they represents the totality of persons. The Yoruba people of Nigeria regard names as having special power. Names are chosen with great care because such names may represent one's prayer to God, to the divinities. It may be expression of faith in the existence of *God (Orunbe)*, God's goodness (*Chukwu dima*), God's providence(*'Yiopese*), and God's love (*Olufemi*).[58] Names may represent the parents' experience in life or during birth. Most of the time names are not just given without special meanings. This is also true among the Ibos of Nigeria.[59] The very important and elaborate ritual called naming ceremony, performed among the Yoruba people of Nigeria signifies how important names are among them. It is also believed that the type of names given to a person may change his or her destiny. Since names represent the totality of what a person is, it is believed that if you know the actual names and appellation of a person, you can make him dance to your wish. Hence, when I was growing up in my village that if a stranger or someone unknown to you calls your name, one should not answer because one's heart may be taken. I believe that African indigenous churches, by placing so much emphasis on names and the inclusion of these names of God, angels, and persons in their reading of Psalms, are making effective use of the African concept of names and power. In order to demonstrate these special powers in the names of God and the Bible, these evangelists and prophets recommend the use of these names in conjunction with the reading of specific Psalms. Different names of God are used in the Old Testament and New Testament. Christians and disciples are asked to pray in the name of Jesus and whatever is asked in Jesus' name shall be given. Although there are some strange and mysterious names, total condemnation of this practice should be avoided especially when God's names are included. African Christians are comfortable using these names that are believed to have abundant powers.

The Use of Medicine

The use of protective Psalms with medicine is an important aspect of the prescription for protection, success and healing. This includes the use of herbs, part of living and non-living things in conjunction with the reading of specific Psalms, burning of candles, prayers and recitation of the names of God for certain number of times. The classification of Psalms into protective, therapeutic Psalms are done according to the African ways of classification of medicine. The truth is that most of the herbs used contain some potent ingredients in themselves that heal diseases. The use of non-living things may not contain any special ingredient for healing, but from my interview, I could gather that the use of those non-living parts like sand, stone, and others is a demonstration of faith in God's power to make those things potent. It is also a demonstration of God's power over nature. What makes the entire materials, including the Psalms, potent for healing is the demonstration of God's power and mercy. It means therefore, that once they are blessed, God transfers that power into anything that the prophets lay their hands on.

The use of herbs and other materials therapeutically does not only have African cultural basis, it also has a biblical basis. II Kings chapter 4 shows that Elisha healed the Shunammite's boy with simply the words in form of prayer. He healed those who ate the poisonous herbs by casting a "meal" to be eaten into the pot (II Kings 4.38-49). The flowing water from river Jordan was also prescribed for Naaman to dip himself 7 times and he was healed (II King 5.14). The Prophet Isaiah prescribed a lump of figs for Hezekiah with the combination of prayers for his boil and he was healed (II Kings 20.1-11).

In the New Testament, Jesus healed the sick with

variety of methods. He healed a leper with mere pronouncement of potent words, "...be thou clean," and a touch (Matt. 8.3). He healed those who were possessed with evil spirit with the mere word, "Go." A blind man was also healed with saliva, clay, water and potent words (Jn. 9.6-7). After washing in the water of Siloam, the blind man's eyes were opened. Paul, the apostle also demonstrated the use of potent words. He healed Publius who was sick of fever and bloody flux (Acts. 28.8). Peter also healed Aeneas by the use of words and the name of Jesus.[60]

The Use of the Power of Words.

I have discussed above the importance of the use of potent words for healing purposes, protection, and success. Since the early missionaries condemned the use of the so-called incantation for these purposes, Africans who became Christians found an alternative. I have also mentioned above that the most logical place to search for the alternative is the Christian Bible, which, they believe, must have potent words for everyday problems of Africans. It is believed that the white man was probably hiding those potent words from African Christians so that they may not be as powerful as they were.

The contents of some books of Psalms resemble that of African potent words for healing, for protection and success. They memorized them and used them for these purposes. In the process, they found them effective. One important revelation during my interview is that there was no iota of doubt as to the potency of the words of Psalms if one knows how, when, and the place to read for specific problems. In the New Testament, African Indigenous Churches in Nigeria found that Jesus Christ used the word of God successfully to overcome Satan. When he was tempted he used the word of God, 'It is written, man shall not live by bread alone, but every word that proceeded out of the mouth of God' (Matt. 4.4 KJV). During the second temptation Jesus used the word of God, 'It is written again, thou shall not tempt the Lord thy God' (Matt. 4.7). During the third temptation he said, Get Thee hence, Satan: for it is written, Thou shall worship the Lord thy God and him only shall thou serve' (Matt. 4.8). There are many other passages where Jesus used the word of God to cast out demons. Paul the apostle used the words of mouth to rebuke and blindfold the enemy, a sorcerer, and a child of the devil, when he was obstructing him (Acts. 13.9-11).

At a glance, the above approaches to Psalms are prone to condemnation as paganistic, magical, and syncretistic, but a critical examination of the practice will show that it came as a result of the fact that Western culture no longer commands awe and admiration as it used to be and they had to search for true original Christianity to deal with the old and new African problems. The discussion above is a perfect example of contextualization at work and Africans' attempt to make their own contribution to Christianity. In doing this, Indigenous African Christians recognizes the fact that God's revelation at all times has never failed to take seriously, the culture of the people in order to make them understand his message. In the Old Testament, the culture of Ancient Near East was taken seriously and used for communication to the people of Ancient Israel. During the Greco-Roman period, the Greco-Roman culture was used for the presentation of the gospel. African indigenous Christians have taken into consideration African religio-cultural tradition in presenting the message of God since the Bible must be made to speak to the life and thought of the people in languages and images that are comprehensible to them. The African culture, customs, traditions, arts, metaphors and images of Africans are necessary for African to feel at home with the gospel. This is important because African religio-cultural traditions is closer to the biblical and ancient Near Eastern culture than the Western culture as affirmed by David Barret: " Africanism is not only good in itself, but also a culture closer than European to the biblical way of life, and therefore more suitable for building a Christian society."[61]

One important fact that must be mentioned is that the African Indigenous Churches in Nigeria that are using this method are growing at a geometrical rate compared with that of the main line missionary churches. Ironically, while the authorities of the mainline churches have condemned these indigenous churches for approaching the Bible this way, many of their members join these churches. In fact, many outstanding church members of the main line churches prefer to keep their membership intact with the missionary churches, but do frequently visit the pastors, and prophets of these African indigenous churches. Testimonies of members and none members who visit these churches either at night or daytime is a powerful evidence of the effectiveness of the use of the Bible this way.

Conclusion

The above shows that the western scholars' division of Psalms into various types may not be relevant to African Christianity. The preoccupation with the authorship and dates, the documentary theories, redactionary theories and others may also not work well with African Christianity. The type of classification in African context is really based not entirely, on the contents of the Psalms, and in addition, on the functions and the efficacy of each portion of the Psalms to protect, heal and obtain, success in African context. The justification of the above approaches to the study of Psalms by African indigenous churches in Nigeria is not only its effectiveness, but also religio-cultural and Near Eastern culture. The fact is that African Christians, in Africa, do not face the same problems as the western Christians. They need different hermeneutics that takes into cognizance, their cultural tradition and the Bible to solve their problems.

The above shows that African indigenous Christians are not passive receivers of Christianity. They made use of whatever they learned from the Western missionaries and adapted it to suit their worldview. African Indigenous Churches have displayed a closer look at the African worldview and they have a closer tie to the spirit-world than the missionary churches. They have presented to the world the most indigenous expression of Christianity in Africa. They have made some substantial contribution to the African interpretation of Christian theology through their emphasis on the wholeness of life, community, healing, the reality of spiritual forces, realistic church worship and prayer power.

Admittedly, care must be taken so as not to have the wrong impression that all aspects of African cultural tradition are good. African Christians must be able to sieve what is good and compatible, and throw away whichever is not compatible. This explains the need for deeper study of African cultural tradition and all aspects of African Indigenous Churches so that the world can learn from them and assist to correct what appears to be wrong. This is an important task that needs to be accomplished. Western Christians, with abundance of resources and advanced civilization, should contribute whatever they can to develop authentic African Christianity. These contribution may be in form of assistance in training young people who are ready to do further researches in this area of African indigenous culture and Christianity. This type of contribution may be in form of exchange of scholars who are interested in working on this aspect of African Christianity.

The research in this area of African Christianity is preliminary. Further work in this area is needed urgently.

Endnotes

[1] I would like to acknowledge the fact that this essay on African cultural hermeneutics would have been impossible without the assistance of the Centre for the Study of Christianity in the Non-Western World, University of Edinburgh, Edinburgh, who offered me a research fellowship in 1996/97. This essay was formerly published in *Vernacular Hermeneutics* (Sheffield: Sheffield Academic Press, 1999), 66-90

[2] This is not an attempt to blame the Christian missionaries for African woes. Despite all the mistakes that Christians missionaries have made, it is an indisputable fact that they have been immense blessing to Africa is in the area of education. They did not only translate the Bible into African languages, they also taught Africans how to read the Bible in their languages and "with their own eyes." This enables African Christians to read the Bible with their own cultural perspectives. Justin Ukpong, " Reading the Bible with African Eyes," *Journal of Theology for Southern Africa (JTSA)*, (June 1995),3-14.

[3] Ibid.,5
[4] ibid., 6
[5] This is what Yorke calls Afrocentic Hermeneutics which is very legitimate since all interpretations and theologies are perspectival. Gosnell L. Yorke, "Biblical Hermeneutics:an Afrocentric Perspective,"*Journal of Religion and Theology*, vol 2, no 2(1995), 145-158.
[6] Justin Ukpong, "Re-reading the Bible," 6.
[7]
[8] Ibid.
[9] Yorke, "Biblical Hermeneutics..," 142-158
[10] R.S Sugirtharajah, (ed) *Vernacular Hermeneutics*.
[11] Arthur Weiser, *The Psalms, Old Testament Library*, trans. By Herbert Hartwell (Philadelphia: the Westmister Press, 1962), 19.
[12] *Out of Depths: the Psalms Speak for us Today* (Philadelphia: The Westminster Press, 1974),5
[13] Weiser, *The Psalms*,19.
[14] Ibid.,20
[15] P.A Dopamu, *Esu: The Invisible Foe of Man* (Ijebu-Ode: Shebiotimo Publications, 1986), 57.
[16] S. Ademiluka, "The Use of Psalms in African Context," M.A Thesis, University of Ilorin, 1991.
[17] Claus Westermann, *Praise and Lament in the Psalms*, translated by K.R Crim and Richard N Soulen (Atlanta: John Knox Press, 1981), 52,64.
[18] Chief J,O Ogunfuye, *The Secrets of the Uses of Psalms* (Ibadan: Ogunfuye Publication, n.d),37
[19] Ibid., 66
[20] Ibid., 7 (now the *Secrets*).
[21] J.A Bolarinwa, *Potency and Efficacy of Psalms* (Ibadan: Oluseyi Press, n.d), 8.
[22] J. Ubrurhe, " Life and Healing Processes in Urhobo Medicine," *Humanitas* (1994) vol. 1, New Series, forth coming.

Endnotes

[23] Ibid.
[24] Ibid.
[25] J.O Mume, *Traditional Medicine in Nigeria* (Agbarho: Jom Tradomedical Naturopathic Hospital ,1978), 65. Eight therapeudic methods in Urhobo medicine are mentioned by Mume.
[26] Ademiluka, "The Use of Psalms in African Context," 80
[27] *Secrets*, 72-73.
[28] *Saint Michael Prayer Book* (Lagos: Neye Ade & Sons, 1988), 21.
[29] Ibid.,
[30] Ibid.,
[31] J. A. Bolarinwa, *Potency and Efficacy of Psalms*, 9.
[32] Prophet Sam Akin Adewole, *The Revelation of God for 1992 and the Years Ahead* (Lagos: Sam Adewole, 1991), 22.
[33] Ogunfuye, *Secrets*, 5-6
[34] Bolarinwa, *Potency and Efficacy of Psalms*, 7
[35] Ibid., 67.
[36] *St Michael Prayer Book*, 15
[37] Ademiluka, "The Use of Psalms," 88
[38] T.N Adeboyejo, *St. Michael Prayer Book*, 23.
[39] Ibid., 14.
[40] S.A Adewole, *Awake Celetians, Satan is Nearer* (Lagos; Celetia Church of Christ, Opopo-Igbala, Ikola Rd, 1991) 45-45.
[41] *The Revelation of God for 1992* (Lagos: Celetia Church of Christ, 1991),24.
[42] Adeboyejo, 27.
[43] *Secrets*, 88-89
[44] Adeboyejo, 31
[45] Secrets, 3-4
[46] Ibid.,69.
[47] Ibid., 43
[48] Some of the contents of these Psalms have been discussed and quoted previously.
[49] The name *Jehovah Jireh* means God the provider and is to be used for special prayer to seek God's favor by reading Psalm 123.
[50] This name means God is righteous and should be used for deliverance when afflicted by principalities and
powers. It should be combined with the reading of Psalm 88. The name should be chanted 7 times.
[51] Means Yahweh Heals (Ex. 15.26) and should be used for sick persons using clear rain water in the calabash
with new palm tree leaves that points to the sky and with 7 candles round the calabash.
This name means God is my shepherd and to be chanted 7 times with the reading of Psalm 23 for protection

[52] God is the provider.
[53] Means God is my shepherd.

Endnotes

⁵⁴It means God of judgment. Call this name 7 times for those who hated and oppressed you unjustly with the reading of Psalm 12.

⁵⁵God is righteous.

⁵⁶ The fact is that some of these names are not invented, they are biblical names in Hebrew.

⁵⁷ In the Old Testament, the proclamation of the names of God (Yahweh) is very frequent and is associated with
His presence and power. See Psalms 29; 28.1; 82; 89.6ff.; 103.20; 148. lff.;, 46.7; 48.8;59.5;69.6; 76.1; 111.9;
54.1; 20.1; Isa.6.2f.; Ikings 2219;Ex.7.4; 12.41;Num. 10.36; I Sam. 17.45; II Sam. 6.2. See more list of those passages in Arthur Weiser, *77, Psalms, 19*

⁵⁸Unfortunately, most of the early missionaries to Africa did not care to understand the importance of these African names, but made us change our names at random. If they had understood these names, I believe that they would have taught us to choose the equivalent in the Old Testament because there are equivalece in the Old Testament.

⁵⁹ For further details about the significance of names, consult Roland Agoro, *Sixteen Names of God* (Ibadan:Olapade Agoro Investment Co.Ltd, 1984.

⁶⁰ I have discussed earlier the efficacy of the use of water, fasting, and faith in African indigenous culture.

⁶¹ *Schism and Renewal in Africa* (Oxford University Press, 1968), 166.

AFRICAN BACKGROUND OF AFRICAN AMERICAN HERMENEUTICS[1]

Introduction

In the summer of 1986 when African Americans gathered in Collegeville to share their experiences in the White colleges, universities, and seminaries, I had the privilege to participate in this groundbreaking meeting. Since then the desire to write this article started forming in my mind. I could not write this article for inclusion in the book (*Stony the Road we Trod:African American Biblical Interpretation*)[2] that came out as a result of the consultation because I had to accept a teaching position at the University of Ilorin, Nigeria. I am, therefore very delighted to present this article. As people say, "it is better late than never."

This essay is as a result of my observation and participation in African American churches, teaching in their college, and reading many of African American writings. My personal experience in Africa (Nigeria, and Kenya) and America (I have the privilege to live in USA for 11 years) is an important factor in deciding to include this chapter. Moreover, I consider Africans in the continent and African Amerians as Africans. The only difference is that we Africans living in the continent of Africa came by air, while the majority of African Americans came by boat. This essay therefore, is not an attempt to glorify either African or African American past, but to bring to a coherent form the genius of African Diaspora in America. Furthermore, to defuse the widespread rumors that African Americans have completely lost their original culture due to the Middle Passage, and suffering they were subjected to in America. Although such myth is gradually dying, it is still our responsibility to repair the damages it has done in the minds of African Americans. There are too many evidences affirming the contrary that are visible to their brothers from Africa who care to observe and learn the ways ofAfrican Americans.[3]

In this paper I want to demonstrate how African cultural hermeneutics has shaped African American Hermeneutics. This will confirm the belief that the actual strength of African American Christianity today is not due to any White or Black missionary activities, but as a result of "independent clandestine meetings where they adapted their African Traditional Religion (very close to that of Old Testament) into a profoundly creative and authentic Christian faith."[4]

African Cultural Hermeneutics and African American Hermeneutics

This section is an attempt to define what I mean by African cultural hermeneutics and African American Hermeneutics.[5] What is African cultural hermeneutics? African cultural hermeneutics in biblical studies is an approach to biblical interpretation that makes African social cultural context a subject of interpretation.[6] It means that African cultural hermeneutics, like any other Third World Hermeneutics, is contextual Hermeneutics since it is always done in the perspective of a particular context. It means that the analysis of the text is done from the perspective of African world-view and culture.[7] African cultural hermeneutics is "re-reading the scripture from a premeditatedly Africa centered perspective" with the purpose of not only understanding the Bible and God in our African experience and culture, but also with the hope of "breaking the Hermeneutical hegemony and ideological stranglehold that Eurocentric biblical scholars have long enjoyed in their interpretation of the Bible."[8] This is a methodology that reappraises ancient biblical tradition and African world-view, culture, and life experience with the purpose of "correcting the effect of the cultural ideological conditioning to which Africa and Africans have been subjected."

The conditions for African cultural hermeneutics have been discussed in the previous chapter that includes being an insider and knowing and living African culture. An interpreter must be a person of faith and believe in the power of the word of God. I will not like to repeat myself here. For full detail see the section on African cultural hermeneutics in the previous chapter.

African American Hermeneutics

What is African American Hermeneutics? In order to answer this question it is necessary to examine how African American scholars/preachers have wrestled with it. Although the literature on methods of interpretation of the Bible generally is staggering,[9] the ones that deal directly with African cultural hermeneutics and African American Hermeneutics are very few in comparison with the ones that are Eurocentric. The few literature on biblical interpretation that are Africentric are mainly concerned with African American preaching styles and interpretative tradition. They include *Black Preaching* by H.H Mitchell;[10] Proclamation *Theology* by J.A Johnson, Jr[11]; *Interpreting the Bible in the Black Church* by Warren A Stewart Sr;[12] Unexpected *News* by Robert McAfee Brown;[13] *Stony the Road We Trod* edited by Cain Hope Felder;[14] *Black Biblical Studies* by Charles B. Copher which has an article, "African Americans and Biblical Hermeneutics: Black Interpretation of the Bible."[15] I also have to wrestle with whether to call it African American Cultural Hermeneutics or simply African American Hermeneutics. I have decided to leave that debate for future research.

Hermeneutics is the principle of interpretation of the Bible. Under this broad definition, it means the methods of interpretation in history which include allegorical method, literal methods, source criticism, literary criticisms, historical criticism, form criticism, traditio oral criticism, textual criticism, redaction criticism, canonical criticism, structural criticism, narrative criticism, social criticism, rhetorical criticism, canonical criticism and other criticism. Though all these methods are honest attempts by Eurocentric scholars to understand the Bible in their own Eurocentric worldview or culture, they do not adequately meet the need of the African and African American people. This is because Africans and African Americans have different experiences from the Eurocentric people. This is the experience of having been beaten, stolen, and uprooted from their homeland and forced to labor without pay in a strange land called America.

African Americans had to use their genius to redefine their own peculiar Hermeneutics with a task of interpreting the Bible in their own ways to meet their needs. These African American redefinitions of Eurocentric Hermeneutics are evident mainly in the ways they sing, chant, read, preach, and interpret the Bible. The undisputed truth is that African American preachers are the authentic scholars who demonstrate African American Hermeneutics that has been handed down from generation to generation. Thus Mr. Mason says,

> It is the black preacher and the black mother, steeped in the true meaning of Christian nurture, which have been God's leading Hermeneutical agents in America. What they have said has been in the style of symbolic and poetic modes of thought. The validity of this style as a medium of God's revelation has been the work of form and literary critics. The black Hermeneutical agent caught a glimpse of the New Hermeneutics before it was academically formalized and in so doing, gave validity to the assumptions of this paper.[16]

Mason believed that sometimes Hermeneutics is used synonymously with the word exegesis, but has come to mean "the study of the laws and principle of interpretation in general." He believes that there is a black Hermeneutics and gave three assumptions for black Hermeneutics:

> (1) There has been a black Hermeneutics and it has a great significance to the study of Hermeneutics,
> (2) The black experience in America is important for the study of Hermeneutics and
> (3) That the cornerstone of Christian education of black people has been preaching.[17]

Bishop Joseph A. Johnson Jr. gave a summary of the section of his book as:

> One may summarize this section of Hermeneutics as follows. Hermeneutics is exegesis, commentary, translation, interpretation, self-understanding, text, interrogation and language. It is Fuch's definition of Hermeneutics as translation into language that speaks today that makes possible the transition to a discussion of Hermeneutics as wrestling with the will and word of God.[18]

The Bishop also gave twelve steps of black Hermeneutics. The principle are listed by Dr. Charles Copher in his book, *Black Studies*:[19]

> (1) Adequate preparation devotionally and prayerfully before one encounter the reading of the Bible.
> (2) One must read the entire book where the text to be interpreted is located.
> (3) Understand the stories before the text and after the text.
> (4) Ask the question about what the problems and the situation of the participants in the story.
> (5) Read the passages aloud so that the text will speak to you as one hears it.
> (6) Discovery of both divine and human element in the situation.
> (7) "You must see what the writer saw, and feel what the participants in the story felt and hear what they heard."
> (8) "Use your imagination and put yourself in the place of the

writer and participants of the story."
(9) "Assume the different roles of the principal characters in the story and act as if you were present when the story was first told."
(10) "Ask yourself this question, 'What special message does this passage of Scripture bring to your people for their healing and renewal?'"
(11) "Wait for God's voice speaking."
(12) "When you preach, go slow, rise high, strike fire and sit down."

The Bishop continues with four other principles of African American Hermeneutics:
1. "The Christian gospel must be proclaimed in a vernacular of the people and the commentary on Scripture must come out of the Black Experience."
2 "God is the creator, sustainer, redeemer of the world and man and he actively is engaged in the work of liberation."
3. Jesus Christ is the revelation of the power, wisdom, and love of God. He is actively engaged in a ministry of healing, liberation and reconciliation."
4. The life, ministry, death and resurrection of Jesus has radically transformed the human situation and has made possible triumphant Christian living."
Dr. Robert Bennett defines Hermeneutics as a " means to translate, to transmit, and to interpret."[20]

From the above there is a basic unanimity among African American scholars in what we call African American Hermeneutics and the basic task of African American Hermeneutics. African American Hermeneutics is, therefore the method of interpretation of the Bible that takes into serious consideration African American experience and culture from generation to generation. As Mitchell said, African American Hermeneutics is the "unique thoughts and interpretations of the Bible that grow out of the Black religious experience and is expressed in Black preaching.[21] The definition above shows that because of the lack of "fruitful contact with Whites and their churches, African Americans were left free to do their own translation into the form of their own world, largely unhampered by the Teutonic captivity of White theology." At this point, the fact that African Americans and the White Americans were in the same geographical location does not matter. Segregation was the order of the day, and this enabled them to be in charge of their own churches and Bible interpretation.

Types of African American Hermeneutics

Liberative Hermeneutics

By liberative Hermeneutics I mean the attempt to use the document of religion to liberate one from all kinds of oppression. What are used to free one from the evil of oppression may be potent words, amulets, herbal medicine (in the case of Africans), and the Bible (in the case of African Indigenous Churches and African Americans). Raymond E. Brown calls this "advocacy Criticism."[22] Bishop Thomas Hoyt. Jr. will probably call this "praxis-liberating methodology"[23]

Let us examine how African American ancestors from time immemorial made use of liberative Hermeneutics to liberate themselves from all kinds of oppressions from the evil ones. In African Traditional Society, the existence of evil ones like witches, enemies, sorcerers, wizards, evil spirits, and all ill wishers is painfully real. The consciousness of these enemies is a major source of fear and anxiety. All evil and pain have causes and are painfully attributed to the above-mentioned ill wishers. Among the Yoruba people of Nigeria, there is a belief that every person has at least one known or unknown enemy called *ota*. Two major types of enmity are visible among the traditional Yoruba people. The first enmity is caused by some perennial quarrels, which come from a variety of circumstances such as land disputes, property inheritance, chieftaincy title disputes and constant rivalries among wives in polygamous homes. Those involved in these disputes are constant enemies of one another and are ready to fight to death. The second type of enemy is called *Aye* (literally means the world). These are sorcerers, witches and all persons who are inherently wicked and malicious by nature. They are more dreadful than the first group of enemies. They go to the extent of employing professional medicine man to harm their enemies. Various techniques are used in harming their enemies. The use of potent words (so-called incantations) pronounced on charms such as *epe*, *(*curse*)*, *isaasi*, *apeta*, *ironsi* and *eedi*.[24] The result of those things can be painful. It may be abnormal behavior, sudden loss of children and property, chronic illness and even death.

The belief in enemies as the main source of all evil and bad occurrences is so strong that nothing happens naturally without some spiritual forces behind it. Thus it is believed that incidents like infant mortality, bareness in women, impotence in men, accidents of any kind, dullness in school children and all other bad things are attributed to different kinds of enemies. Constant fear and insecurity may also be caused by hostile environment other than malignant forces, but also from events such as road and fire accidents, gunshot and cutlass. People, therefore, do go to liberate themselves from such enemies.

Before the advent of Christianity, Africans had a cultural way of dealing with the problem of enemies and all evil ones. There are various techniques for making use of natural materials and potent words of mouth, (incantations) which they put to defensive and offensive use in dealing with evil ones in order to liberate themselves from such powerful enemies.

The use of imprecatory potent words of mouth (the so-called incantations or *ogede* in Yoruba language) is considered an effective way to liberate one from evil. Traditionally when an African identifies an enemy and does not have the potent words or medicine to deal with such enemy, a person consults a medicine man (*babalawo* or *onisegun* or *oologun* in Yoruba language) that prepares or teaches the person some potent words or gives a charm for liberation from an attack of the enemy.

Another major way of obtaining protection against enemies mentioned above in African societies is the use of charms or amulets. Amulets and charms are usually obtained from medicine men that are healers and diviners. They are used for diverse purposes but mainly as protective devices to prevent enemies, witches and wizards, evil spirits from entering a house and attacking a person. It can be used to nullify all the oppressive attempts of enemies or sorcerers. They are prepared with different ingredients according to the purpose of the charm or amulets.

African converts to Christianity were forbidden to practice African cultural ways of liberating one self from an enemy because the missionaries labeled them as paganistic and abominable to God. But unfortunately the type of Western Christianity brought by the missionaries gave no substitute for protection.[25] More unfortunate is the fact that what Western Christianity introduced to Africans did not reveal the secrets of Western power and knowledge. Instead it revealed prejudice and oppression in the missionary support for colonial masters. African Christians began to feel that there must be more in such a popular White man's religion that missionaries did not give to them since it did not meet the present need of the Africans by liberating them from the oppression of the evil ones. African indigenous Christians sought vigorously for that hidden treasures not revealed to them in the missionary religion. They sought it in the Bible in their own way and in their own culture. Using African cultural hermeneutics to interpret the Bible, they found that secret power in the Bible, especially in the book of Psalms. They use the Bible protectively, therapeutically, and successfully in order to fill the gap left by the Eurocentric Christianity.[26]

When Africans were stolen, raped, and forced to sail across the Atlantic, they were already well immersed in this liberative Hermeneutics from their forefathers. Despite all the oppressive policies to strip them of their culture, this liberative Hermeneutics still survived up till today. The slavers could "change the length of hoes, the manner of cultivating crops," the names of the African slaves, but they could not strip them off their African culture. They could not change the way they sang, prayed, and read the Bible.[27] Africans in America were not only forcibly brought to that country and completely cut off from their past, writing and reading, "common language by intermixing persons of different African tribes," were forbidden. They were forbidden to be Africans and yet never allowed to be Americans. What a dilemma!!! Despite all the oppression, socially, psychologically, economically and politically, it has always been amazing to me that African Americans have "displayed a tremendous transcendent spirit that has enabled them to confront the Bible creatively."[28]

Liberative methodology "uses the interpretative principle of experience in religious, social, political, and economic arenas." When one surveys the experience of the African Americans in the United States, one can readily understand the strong influence of African culture and the dynamics of language that have been stressed in the interpretation of the Scripture.[29] The African American experience in the homeland and in a strange land, called America, has conditioned their interpretation of the Bible in America. Just as African American ancestors believed that there must be power in the book (Bible) that belong to those who colonize them, and that such power in the religion and book of the colonizer were hidden from them, so also African Americans associated power with the book of the slavers (Bible) who did not only colonize their ancestors, but forcibly brought them to America. They sought to use the power in that book to combat oppression by the slavers. They interpreted the book to bring out that power against their slavers who are regarded as enemies and evil incarnate embodied in witches and wizards in their original home in Africa. By their acts of oppression, racism, slavery, and others, they the African Americans saw them as the enemies used by the evil spirits that fills the American forest, water, hills and trees. The Bible therefore becomes an instrument of liberation.

Credit must be given to James Cone whom I

consider the champion of reading the Bible liberatively.³⁰ When he reads the text of the Bible, what he finds is liberation from oppression. To him what the Bible is all about or the basic theme of the Bible is liberation or salvation from all evil. He insists that Christian theology is a theology of liberation. To him "God came in Christ to set the captive free."³¹ Other African American scholars who also made important contribution to the liberative Hermeneutics are: Martin Luther King, Jr. with the theme of love of God, Christ, and human beings; J. Deotis Roberts reconciliation through liberation; Joseph Washington, Jr. with the theme of blacks as God's chosen people; Albert Cleage with the theme Jesus the black Messiah; Major Jones with freedom and salvation in the context of love; Cecil Cone with the theme of an Almighty Sovereign.³²

Speaking of how African Americans took the Bible so seriously, H.H Mitchell says correctly,

> They took the Bible extremely seriously, but they never condoned slavery. Their spirituals attest to the fact that they seized on the Moses narrative and sang, 'tell ol Pharaoh to let my people go!' When they sang about 'stealing away', they no doubt had some notion of the prayer closet, but there is strong reason to believe that to steal away to Jesus was also to escape to freedom! Similarly, to sing 'I ain't got long to stay here' is not exclusively other worldly escape. It is the code language of the gospel of **self-liberation.**³³

Hoyt. Jr. is also correct when he says:

> Blacks tend to share a perspective on the Bible that celebrates God's liberating action in history. Traditionally, this liberation has centered on salvation from the power of sin and evil, but there has always been a parallel emphasis for blacks on salvation from the evil concretized in racial exclusivity and the dehumanization of the poor. Perhaps because of the real effect of the brutality of slavery, segregation, and discrimination, blacks share a common ethos of salvation in which the biblical story speaks naturally to their story. This is what some call 'the Hermeneutical privilege of the poor and

African American Hermeneutics

oppressed'."³⁴

The majority of the sermons preached by African American fathers were sermons of liberation. A close examination of "An Ante-bellum Sermon," which David T. Shannon analyzes in his essay, "'An Ante-bellum Sermon': A Resource for an African American Hermeneutics," show that the sermon is liberative in method and theme. For example in lines 9-22 of the sermon:

> Now ole Pher'oh, down in Egypt,
> Was de wuss man evah bo'n,
> An' he had de Hebrew chillun
> Down dah wukin' in his co'n;
> T well de Lawd got tiached o' his folllin',
> an' sez he: "I'll let him know-
> Look hyeah, Moses, go tell Pher'oh
> Fu' to let dem chillun go."
>
> "An' ef he refuse to do it,
> I will make hi rue de houah
> Fu' I'll empty doen on Egypt
> All de vials o my powah."
> Yes he did-an' dPher'oh's ahmy
> Was n't wuth a ha'f a dime.³⁵

Lines 23-36 which express the general theme of a trust in God, for God will send a liberator is also liberative in its interpretation and theme.

> Fu' de Lawd will lhe'p his chillun
> You kin trust him evah time
> An' yo'enemies may 'sail you
> In de back an'in de front;
> But de Lawd is all aroun' you
> Fu' to ba'de battle's brunt.
> Dey kin fo'ge yo' chains an' shackles
> F'om de mountains to de sea
> But de Lawd will sen' some Moses
> Fu' to set his chillun free.
> An' de lan' shall hyeah his thundah
> Lak a blas' f'om Gab'el's ho'n,
> Fu' de Lawd of hosts is mighty
> When he girds his ahmor on.³⁶

Theopoetic Hermeneutics

By theopoetic Hermeneutics, I mean the act of reading and interpreting religion poetically. This may involve all kinds of melody such as chanting, singing, dancing and producing any form of music. This is the reading, chanting, singing the scripture as the word of God. Reading and interpreting religion theopoetically may aid the reader and interpreter to see and understand religion better. It is capable of bringing some unique revelation which otherwise would have not been revealed to the reader or interpreter. By theopoetic, I mean songs of God or song to God.

In African traditional society, religion, politics, economy, are interpreted theopoetically. In our culture, music, chanting, dancing is part of everyday life. There is scarcely anything done without it. In the time of joy and sorrow, some music or rhythmic symbolic acts are performed. Religion is celebrated and interpreted theopoetically. Music is an integral part of all aspect of life in Africa and it serves diverse function as performed by the individual and groups and the community.[37] Music in African traditional society symbolizes "vitality" and sense of "aliveness." In time of death, funeral songs are sung. Dirges are common songs to express sorrow. When the land is being cultivated, work songs and dance are offered by certain age groups to aid faster cultivation. When there is no rain and the crops are not doing well, some ritual songs and dances are offered to appease the gods to bring rain and good harvest. In the time of new harvest, ritual dance and songs are rendered as an expression of gratitude to the gods. Perhaps, it will be correct to say that Africans sing and dance their religion.

I grew up in a remote village, which I can say represents a typical traditional African society. The village is called Irunda, in Kogi State, Nigeria. I watched with amazement how people responded to both secular and religious music and dance. At times people threw money to dancers and musicians. When money is not available, some women and men would give their gold necklaces, beautiful attires, such as *agbada,* to the singers or dancers. The power in the words sung, chanted, or pronounced in rhythmic form is unbelievable. African priests chant, sing and dance to receive an oracle from the gods or spirits. In traditional African society, most potent words are chanted or songs for effective release of power. I remember very vividly in 1963, my age mate came to my late brother's farm for cultivation of heaps. They were about 30 in number. The leader of the group is called *soje.* He was supposed to be able to cultivate more heaps than all of them. The singer or the man employed to chant the names of each person in the group, especially, *soje.* It is expected that if anyone in the group fell behind, the singer would go after him and sing or chant his name. That afternoon, the singer came after me and started chanting my cognomen (*Oriki* in Yoruba language of Nigeria):

> *Attesogun, Asogun jengbele*
> *Atesogun, Asogun jengbele*
> *Omo a ro'so mo pa dei enini*
> *Omo a mu bibo gbarigidi ese*
> *Omo moja moja we mu dadara ponra*
> *Ko se ma ja nko*
> *Ori omo nain a dun pepere pepere pepere*

Translation

> A son that ties cloth without caring of the dew
> That does not care about what happens
> A son was told not to fight but he carries sword
> What if you are going to fight?
> People's heads would be rolling on the floor

Athough I did not belong to that group, the song had a dramatic effect on me. Eventually I was able to cultivate more heaps than I usually did. Perhaps, it will not be an exaggeration to say that in traditional Africa, music is everything and everything is music. In my village, there are special songs to announce the time of wrestling festival.

There are special songs for the annual worship of *Olokesi*[38] There is special songs for the coming of the new yam festival, and for the celebration of *egungun*.[39] There are special songs to express hatred and love. There are special songs for politics. There are special for the death of an elderly person. Such songs and dances (called *ite*) become the means by which the philosophy of death is interpreted. In short, there are special songs for every occasion in Africa. An example of a special song for wresting in my village can be sung by the one who wants to wrestles: *E m'egbem ko mi* (give me my age mate), the group will answer: *'Tori 'di mo ti gha* (because I come to wrestle).

Another wresting song says, *O na le gba 'di* (the one who is to be the head of wrestler), the group will respond, *Ouule re gogo nago* (the roof of his house must be very high).

African indigenous churches are consciously aware of the importance of songs and dances in the interpretation of reality in Africa. I had the privilege of conducting a research on the African Indigenous churches in Nigeria. Most of the time during the church services, singing and dancing take more time than any other activities. They preached in songs. They prayed in songs. They danced flamboyantly. Songs and dancing become the means by which the prophets or apostles prophesy. It is not unusual for any person to burst into song at the middle of a sermon in African Indigenous Churches. In such a case, the pastor would stop; join in singing before he continues his sermon after the congregation has finished singing. I also had the privilege of being a radio pastor in Nigeria. We recognized the indispensability of songs if we wanted people to listen to our messages. Messages were rendered in songs, and music. We made provision for a special type of chanting called *ewi*. Sometimes the Bible is chanted. At another time, commentaries on specific text are rendered poetically. We also devised a way to make people listen to our message. A preacher preached for about five minutes and played a song for another five minutes and continued the message for another five minutes then another song. We recognized that listeners wanted the songs but not the messages. We, therefore, made it impossible for anyone to listen to the songs without listening to the messages.

Such is the environment from where African Americans were forcibly uprooted to America. Having been immersed in such worldview and tradition in Africa, they arrived in so strange a land, forbidden to learn how to read and write, to use common African languages for communication, and to beating of drums on the plantation for the reason of avoiding rebellion, African Americans had to devise a different way to survive. Eventually they became ingenuous in their use of symbols. After the terrible dehumanization of slavery, segregation, and discrimination, the African Americans were not converted in significant numbers until the eighteenth century during the revival movements.[40] They responded to the European Evangelical conversion preaching and accepted Christ and the Bible, but not as the slavers accepted it. They accepted it differently and interpreted it differently. They articulated the Bible in their own ways, "in songs, prayers, sermons, testimonies and addresses" that were chanted. This was a way of interpreting the Bible in the light of their African and American experiences. Wimbush put it correctly when he described the way they accepted the Bible: "As the people of God in the Hebrew Bible were once delivered from enslavement, so the Africans sang and shouted, would they be delivered. As Jesus suffered unjustly but was raised from the dead to new life, so they sang, and would they be raised from their 'social death' to new life. So went the songs, sermons, and testimonies."[41] James Johnson, in his description and interpretation of the spirituals, also emphasize how the Bible is interpreted different in a theopoetic language of music:

> At the psychic moment there was at hand therecise religion for the condition in which (African) found himself thrust. Far from his native land and customs, despised by those among whom he lived, experiencing the pang of separation of loved ones on the auction block...(they) seized Christianity, the religion which implied the hope that in the next world there

would be a reversal of conditions...The result was a body of songs voicing all the cardinal virtues of Christianity...through a modified form of primitive African music.... (they) took complete refuge in Christianity, and the Spirituals were literally forged in the heat of religious fervor.... It is not possible to estimate the sustaining influence that the story of the Jews narrated in the Old Testament exerted upon the Negro.
The story at once caught and fired the imaginations of the Negro bards, and they sang, sang their hungry listeners into a firm faith.[42]

The spirituals reflect the process by which the African Americans transformed from the abstract book religion to the practical religion that fits their experience in both worlds. They sang the Bible from moment to moment. Whatever they heard and read were converted to songs to be chanted and danced. Some of these songs were authentic commentaries and criticism of the social situation that the slaves found themselves.[43] As Wimbush has described, some of these "songs, sermons, addresses and exhortations reflect a hermeneutics characterized by a looseness, and even playness, vis-à-vis the biblical texts themselves."[44] He continued to describe such songs, sermons, addresses and exhortation as interpretation of the Bible, which was not controlled, by literal interpretation of the text, but by free imaginations and tradition accustomed to in the African American homeland.

The interpretation was not controlled by the literal word of the texts, but by social experience. The texts were heard more than read; they were engaged as stories that seized and freed the imagination...Many of the biblical stories, themselves the product of cultures with well-established oral traditions, functioned sometimes as allegory, as parable, or as veiled social criticism. Such stories well served the African slaves, not only on account of their well-established oral tradition, but also because their situation dictated veiled or indirect social criticism--'hitting a straight lick with a crooked stick'.[45]

One of the examples of the theopoetic interpretation is the

song,

> Go down, Moses
> Way down in Egypt land,
> Tell ole Pharaoh, Let my people go.
> Dey crucified my Lord
> An' He never sid a mumblin' word.
> Dey crucified my Lord,
> An' He never said a mumblin' word,
> Not a word---not a word--not a word.
> Dey nailed Him to de tree
> An' He never said a mumblin' word.
> Dey nailed H to de tree,
> An' He never said a mumblin' word,
> Not a word--nt a word--not a word.
> Dey pierce Him in de side,
> An' He never said a mumblin' word.
> Dey pierced Him in de side,
> An' He never said a mumblin' word,
> Not a word-not a word-not a word.
> Sometimes I feel like a motherless child,
> Sometimes I feel like a motherless child,
> Sometimes I fell like a motherless child
> A long way from home.[46]

Christa K. Dixton described correctly that the Negro spirituals are songs that become example of how the Word of God can become incarnate and take on flesh in the life of human being. These songs are unique interpretation of the Bible in themselves that reflect the experience of a particular people. An explanation of even a few of the spiritual texts opens up a new and unexpected dimension of understanding about how God's Word can become incarnate, take on flesh, in human-and inhuman-situations, even today. We begin to see that the spirituals are as faith engendering and life affirming for us in our time as they were for the community of believers that originally created, shaped, and preserved them.[47]

    It appears to me as if whenever the African slaves read the Bible, they read it as music or songs. The interpretation of any particular text, therefore, reflects songs of God.

Narrative Hermeneutics

Narrative Hermeneutics is an approach that sees the Bible as storybook and interprets those stories as divine stories. Perhaps, this can be labeled storytelling Hermeneutics. This is closely related to narrative criticism[48] but it is different. While narrative criticism tries to distinguish the real author of the Bible from the implied author, and the real audience from the implied audience, African American narrative Hermeneutics sees the Bible as stories to be told not because of its aesthetic value, but as stories that actually happened as God planned it, and is capable of happening, and in fact, will happen again in their lives. African American Hermeneutics' preoccupation is the African American audience who listens to the stories narrated. To them God is behind the story and will eventually deliver the poor, the feeble, the oppressed black people as He has delivered the oppressed in history. These stories are narrated in poems, and in songs with a vivid imagination.

The background of this narrative style is the African American ancestors' home. In African indigenous society, the major means by which children and adult are taught to be strong, to grow, and to be courageous and wise is through narrative hermeneutics, that is, through stories of what really happened in life. Adult are also taught through proverbs that came out of life experience. When there are quarrels between husband and wife, brothers and sisters, and communities, elders used proverbs and stories for judgment. Different methods are used to narrate these stories and proverbs. Sometimes it is done through songs, beating of drums, and through various symbols. An example of narrating stories through drums readily comes to mind. The Yoruba people of Nigeria are good at this through the talking drum *dundun* or another types of drum known as *bata* or *ogidigbo*. In Yoruba tradition, there are people who are gifted and who specialize in the beating of these types of drums. That is why they say, *Bi owe bi owe la nlu ilu ogidigbo. Ologbon ni njo. Omoran ni si nmo* (we beat the drum called *ogidigbo* in proverbs. Only the wise understands it. Only the skilled knows it.).

The narrative method is one of the most productive ways of imparting, a basic knowledge of existence, as well as teaching courage, strength, good behavior, self-discipline, and persistency. It is an effective way of learning how to make it in life despite difficulties.

I remember very vividly sitting in the moon light in a group, and listening to stories that teach courage and discipline in my village. I remember seating with my mother and brothers listening to stories that taught me good ethical behavior. In fact, in my elementary school days we were taught by our teachers how to formulate and tell stories with lessons starting with, *Ni igba kan, igba kan lo igba kan bo aye duro titi lai lai* (once upon a time, a time comes and a time goes, but the world remains forever.) I used to be able to formulate interesting and thought-provoking and ethical stories and narrate them.

Such is the world of African Americans who were stolen and forced to come to a strange land called America. The world they knew was the world of narrative technique of imparting knowledge, ethic, and courage for survival. When they were converted, they fell in love with the narrative part of the Bible. They were attracted to the adventures of the Hebrews in bondage and how they escaped, the story of the eight century prophets who denounced vehemently the social injustice of the their time. They fell in love with the stories of compassion, passion, and resurrection of Jesus Christ. They told and retold, interpreted, and reinterpreted these stories as their own stories. As the children of Israel were delivered from bondage in Egypt, so also the African Americans would be delivered from the bondage of oppression, segregation, discrimination, and death from the slavers. Thomas Hoyt is right when he says:

African American Hermeneutics

In Black culture the 'story' is taught which establishes the authority of the Bible, for in its story, blacks find the essence of their story in modern life. Blacks are excellent story communicators and in many respects are, as Africans, understandably closely related to the worldview of the ancient Near East.[49]

African Americans read the Bible historically and concretely. African Americans did this so effectively when they told and retold the story of ancient Israel as the liberation story.[50] The story of the three Hebrew 'boys' in the fiery furnace, the story of the dry bones in the valley, the stories of the birth, suffering, sorrow, death, burial and resurrection of Jesus became the story of hope for the African American people.[51] "Through the retelling of the biblical story, and the story of the black man and women in America, the former story may evoke faith in God's activity, but the latter story, when heard and heeded, helps black and white respond more creatively to the divine Word for our present situation."[52]

Orality Hermeneutics

By orality Hermeneutics, I mean the reading and interpretation of a religious text orally. In this there is a need for serious memorization of oral tradition as passed from generation to generation. This is closely connected with narrative or storytelling Hermeneutics that I have just mentioned above. In Africa, the art of reading and writing in the Western concept was not common. It belonged to the professionals. The majority of Africans were not able to read or write the Western way. Yet religious rules and taboos are learned and passed on from generation to generation. Circular codes are taught and memorized. Ethical teaching is given to children and adult in the community through the art of storytelling and they are memorized verbatim. Like the people of ancient Near East, where most of the Bible events took place, Africans by nature are good in passing information orally from generation to generation.

African American Hermeneutics

I had the privilege of attending a Baptist mission elementary school at Irunda. It is amazing that among the first thing they taught us was how to memorize Bible passages. I still remember vividly that even though we did not know how to read or write, we memorized Psalms 1, 8, and 24 very easily in our language. I still remember these Psalms and every time I preach on one of them, my memory flashes back to the time someone was reading those Psalms to me. Up till today many people are still illiterate, in western term, and still learn things orally. Many of the religious rules, and revelation of gods of African indigenous religion are still not committed to systematic writing. Most Ifa priests and priestesses still memorize. Many of motor and motorcycle mechanics, sewing mistresses and other apprentices, still memorize instead of reading books.

Besides the above use of oral methods, words spoken are also considered sacred in Africa. There are words that are considered potent, depending on how, where, and when they are spoken. Oral expression takes on a different form of power if done appropriately. Africans believe that some of these words are potent for healing, for protection, success, and virtually all kinds of situation. That is why some words and oral traditions are not committed to writing. They believe that they will loose their potency if written.

From the above, my reader will agree with me that the African Americans, having been uprooted forcibly from Africa, have a rich history of oral communication. The popular African literatures are tales, proverbs, religious taboos preserved and transmitted orally from generation to generation as mentioned above. By the time Africans were brought here in 1619 as slaves, some trained narrators, or amateur storytellers have taught some of them orally. When Africans were brought here they brought this oral style of historical-cultural transmission with them.[53] Africans who were brought here had to cope with a situation in America where literacy was highly valued and Africanism was forbidden. Africans who were also forbidden to learn how to read or write had to develop a sophisticated oral traditional system to communicate among themselves. I believe that before I. Engnell, E. Nyberg, and the Scandinavian School ever thought of developing traditio oral criticism, Africans and African Americans knew it and had made use of it in their reading and interpretation of the Bible. The majority of the material on African American preaching comes from oral accounts. According to David Shannon, one of the best examples is the collection of James Weldon Johnson's sermon drawn from folk/oral tradition.[54] Zora Neale Hurston sermon, *The Sanctified Church*, is another example of oral African American sermons.[55] According to Shannon, "though we do not have written records of many of the early African American sermons, we do have access to the oral tradition of biblical exposition and interpretation through such works as those belonging to James Johnson, Zora Neale Hurston, Ned Walker, Paul Laurence Dunbar, Ralph Illison, Richard Wright, and James Baldwin."[56] Another possible African American Hermeneutics is the imaginative hermeneutics, which was used for exposition of the Bible in songs, and storytelling fashion. More work is needed on this.

Conclusion and Summary.

What I have done here is to give an outline of African American Hermeneutics and their background from their ancestral home in Africa. I chose to do this not because I think that I am an expert in African American Hermeneutics, but because I have always been fascinated whenever I have the opportunity of listening to African American preachers. It brings to memory the life I lived in my village in Nigeria. I am also fascinated to see that African Americans were able to use their genius to adapt African concepts and ideas to America despite their oppressive situation.

I have discussed liberative, theopoetic, narrative or storytelling, and orality hemeneutics, African Americans combine use of various methodologies. No one method is adequate. All the elements could be found in one interpretation or one sermon.

When the African Americans read the Bible, they read it liberatively. When they chant and sing the Bible, they chant and sing it liberatively. When they read and interpret the Bible, they interpret it like a story (a story of their experience.) When they read the Bible they read and interpret it imaginatively. When they read and interpret the Bible they read it and interpret it as an oral document.

There is still a need to analyze further, these Hermeneutics until it has come to be recognized and appreciated. Imaginative mode of interpreting the Bible still needs further analysis. I hope that African Americans would take it from here and analyze these various Hermeneutics with more intensity.

African American Hermeneutics

Endnotes

¹ This paper is included because I regarded all African Americans as Africans even though they are in America. This is an article read at the Society of Biblical Literature Annual Meeting, Boston, 1999.
²Edited by Cain Hope Felder, (Minneapolis: Fortress Press, 1991).
³ One day when we were having a meeting of African pastors in Dallas, Rev. Lee Turner came to the meeting and said one remarkable word to us. "I am an African. The only difference between me and you is that you came voluntarily and by plane, be I came from Africa by force and by ship." I accepted that words and became very close. I considered all African Americans as Africans. By that I am extending the African boundaries to America as far as history and essence are concerned.
⁴Henry H. Mitchell, *Black Preaching: The Recovery of a Powerful Art* (Nashville: Abingdon Press, 1990),13.
⁵The definition and condition is taken from my earlier article, "African cultural hermeneutics," in *Vernacular Hermeneutics*, 65-86.
⁶Ibid, 5
⁷Ibid, 6
⁸ This is what Yorke calls Afrocentric Hermeneutics which is very legitimate since all interpretations and theologies are perspectival. Gosnell L Yorke, *Journal of Religion and Theology*, vol. 2 no 2 (1995), 145-158.
⁹I will like to mention few Eurocentric books on Hermeneutics: Robert Grand and David Tracy, *A Short History of the Interpretation of the Bible* (Philadelphia: Fortress Press, 1984); Bernard Ramm, *Protestant Biblical Interpretation* (Grand Rapids, Michigan: Baker Book House, 1970); Terence J Keegan, *Interpreting he Bible: A Popular Introduction to Biblical Hermeneutics* (New York: Paulist Press, 1985) Willard Swartley, ed., *Essays on Biblical Interpretation* (Elkhart, Indiana: Institute of Mennonite Studies, 1984); Rogers and Donald K. McKim, *The Authority and Interpretation of the Bible: An Historical Approach* (New York: Harper and Row, 1975).
¹⁰This book has been revised in 1990 and published by Abingdon Press.
¹¹(Shreveport: Fourth Episcopal District Press, 1977).
¹²Valley Forge: Judson Press, 1984).
¹³(Philadelphia: Westminster Press, 1984).
¹⁴This book came as a result of the consultation on African American Hermeneutics and it appears to be the best so far on the subject. Particularly interesting are Dr. V. L Winbush's article, "The Bible and African Americans: An Outline of an Interpretative History," 81-97; Dr. T. Hoyt, Jr.'s article, "Interpreting Biblical Scholarship for the Black Church Tradition," 17-39; W. Myers' article, "The Hermeneutics Dilemma of the

African American Biblical Student," 40-56; and D. Shannon's article, "An Ante-bellum Sermon: A Resource for an African American Hermeneutics," 98-123.

[15](Chicago, Ill: Black Light Fellowship, 1993).

[16]Mason is quoted by Charles Copher in Black *Biblical Studies*, 70.

[17]ibid., 69

[18]ibid., 70.

[19]70-71

[20]William Mason,, "Hermeneutics and the Black Experience," Reformed Review 23(Summer 1970), 4, quoted by Copher in *Black Biblical Studies*, 69.

[21]*Black Preaching*, 17.

[22]*An Introduction to the New Testament* (New York: Doubleday, 1997), 27-28. According to him, the term also extends to, not only the liberationist, but also to "African Americans, Feminist, and related studies.

[23]"Interpreting Biblical Scholarship The Black Church Tradition," in *Stony the Road We Trod*, 24.

[24]P.A Dopamu, " The Reality of Isaasi, Apeta, Ironsi and Efun as forces of Evil among the Yoruba," *Journal Arabic and Religious Studies* 4 Dec. 1987):50-61; Dopamu, "Epe: The Magic of Curse among the Yoruba," *Religions* 8 (Dec.1983), 1-11. Solomon Ademiluka,, "The Use of Psalms in African Context", M.A Thesis, University of Ilorin, Ilorin, Nigeria, Dec. 1990,57.

[25]At a point among the Yoruba people of Nigerian, men who accepted this type of Christianity without arming themselves with African power of Words, amulets, and charms were ridiculed and called women. To them Christianity was an impotent religion.

[26]For more details about how the African Indigenous Churches in Nigeria use the Bible for liberation from oppression of evil ones, see Adamo, *Vernacular Hermeneutics*, 65-86.

[27]Mitchell, *Black Preaching*, 13.

[28]Hoyt, Jr., *Stony the Road We Trod*, 27

[29]Ibid., 24.

[30]*A Black Theology of Liberation* (Philadelphia: Lippincott, 1970); *God of the Oppressed, The Spiritual and the Blues,*

[31]This is an important theme of the Bible. The theme of deliverance, exodus, redemption run through the entire Christian Bible. Only ignorance of the content and theology of the Christian Bible will deny this.

[32]Hoyt, Jr. *Stony the Road We Trod*, 21-22.

[33]*Black Preaching*, 21. The italicization of self-liberation is mine.

[34]Ibid., 28-29.

[35]"'An Ante-bellum Sermon': A Resource for an African American Hermeneutics," in *Stony the Road We Trod*, 10.

[36]Ibid., 110

African American Hermeneutics

[37] Portia K. Maultsby, "Africanism in African American Music," in *Africanism in American Culture*, Joseph E. Holloway (ed) (Bloomington, Indiana: Indiana University Press, 1990), 185-210.
[38] A sacred hill which the villagers believe protect the village of Irunda.
[39] Musquraders.
[40] V.L Winbush, "The Bible and African Americans: An Outline of an Interpretative History," *Stony the Rod We Trod*, 85.
[41] Ibid., 86.
[42] James Weldon Johnson, ed., *The Book of American Negro Spirituals* (New York:Viking Press, 1925), 20,21; See also Wimbush, *Stony the Read We Trod*, 87.

[43] Johnson, ed. *The Book of American Negro Spirituals;* James Cone and Gayraud Wilmore, eds., *Black Theology: A Documentary History, 1966-1979* (Maryknoll, N.Y: Orbis Books, 1979), 227f.
[44] Wimbush, *Stony the Road We Trod*, 89.
[45] Ibid., 88.
[46] Quoted by Wimbush, Ibid., 87-88.
[47] *Negro Spirituals: from the Bible to Folksongs* (Philadelphia: Fortress Press, 1976), X
[48] Raymond E. Brown, *Introduction to the New Testament*, 25-26. See also W.A. Beardslee, *Literary Critic of the New Testament* (Philadelphia: Fortress Press, 1970; M.A. Powell, *What is Narrative Criticism?* (GBSNT Mineapolis: A/F, 1990).
[49] *Stony the Road We Trod*, 25
[50] The most famous of the black preachers storyteller was John Jasper (1812-1902) who was noted for moving his audience to ecstasy with vivid view of heaven. We were told that White as well as Black crowded his church waiting to be moved. He was the founder -pastor of Sixth Mt. Zion Baptist Church in Richmond, Virginia. H.H Mitchell, *Black Preaching*, 70.
[51] *Stony the Road We Trod.*, 29.
[52] Ibid., 31.
[53] Hoyt, Jr., *Stony the Road We Trod*, 26
[54] David Shannon, *Stony the Road We Trod*, 100.
[55] Ibid.
[56] Ibid., 102.

PART II

AFRICAN BIBLICAL STUDIES

Cush as Africa in the Old Testament[1]

Introduction

The purpose of this paper is to examine the various meanings of the word *Cush* that has been put forward by many scholars and propose what I consider to be the most appropriate meaning of the word *Cush*. I will discuss the various advantages and implications for African churches if the word *Cush* is translated as I would suggest. This has also been discussed extensively in my book, *Africa and Africans in the Old Testament*.[2]

The Origin of the word "*Cush*"

It appears to me that the first people to use the word *Cush* are the Africans themselves. The Ancient Egyptians used the word *Cush* or *Kaushu*, or *Kash* to refer to a very limited area of land or tribe beyond Semna and Kerma before it

Cush as Africa in the Old Testament

later extended to include all the lands further south.³ Although the earliest reference known to us is an Egyptian document known as inscription of Ameni dated to the Sixth Dynasty, under Pepi II,⁴ the Annals of Thurtmose III inscribed on the walls of the corridor of the Temple of Amon at Karnak inscribed the word *Cush*.⁵ The stelae of Thutmose IV also recorded the encounter with the "Abominable chief of Cash."⁶ Menhotep I mentioned in his inscription that he sailed up the Nile to *Kesh*.⁷ There are many more records of *Cush* in the Egyptian documents listed in my book, *Africa and Africans in the Old Testament*.⁸

Assyrian records also discussed their encounter with Africans called *Cush*. The annalistic text of Esharhaddon record their military encounter with Kushites and mentioned specifically, King Tirhakah who ruled Egypt during the so-called Kushite Dynasty in Egypt.⁹ In the Dog River Stele which Esharhaddon wrote to commemorate his victory over his enemy, he mentioned *Kusu* and King Tirhaqar.¹⁰ The Hebrews probably learned of the word Cush from the Africans themselves, possibly when they were in Egypt for 430 years. Five times the word Cush appears as names of persons or places. It appears in every strand of Biblical Literature, Law, Prophet and Writings.

Survey of Cushite Activities in the Old Testament

It must be noted that the history of activities of the Cushites is incomplete without the Egyptians just as the history of the Egyptians is incomplete without the history of the Cushites. That is the reason in most cases they are treated together in the Old Testament and in the Assyrian records. They both belong together as Africans. They belong to one race.¹¹ The existence of the Cushites is the existence of the Egyptians as the existence of Egyptians means the existence of the Cushites. The Cushites was the main military police in Egypt.¹² The Egyptians themselves recorded that the Cushites were their ancestors and that the place where Egyptians are staying was originally water. When the sea rescinded the Cushite ancestors went to that portion of the dry land to colonize it.[13] Egypt is the corridor from where other Africans, south of the Sahara traveled outside the known world. A closer look at the map of Africa shows that the continent was surrounded by sea-south, north, east, and west. The Cushite gold and other minerals went out to the ancient known world through Egypt. That was the only place where the Cushite could travel by land to the ancient known world. This means that the Eurocentric propaganda that Egypt had no interaction with the so-called Africa, south of the Sahara, is part of the conspiracy to separate Egypt from the rest of Africa by making Egypt part of Europe. In fact, whenever the Cushite came out through Egypt, the ancient known world always call them Cushite and Egypt simply because it is difficult to differentiate and separate the two.[14]

A very good illustration of this problem is the habit of calling all the people who came from South America to America, Mexicans even though they are from different countries other than Mexico. The survey of Cushite activities that will be discussed below is closely interwoven with that of Egypt. The survey will be some representative passages in the Old Testament, and will emphasize the process of de-Africanization of the Bible by the Eurocentric scholars.

The use of *Cush* as a Name(s) of person.

In the Torah, there are two passages where *Cush* (Gen. 10:6,7, 8; Num. 12:1) was used as identification of names of persons. In the Table of Nations (Gen. 10:1-8) Cush is the first son of Ham. He also had Seba, Havilah, Sabtecha, Raamah, and Nimrod who became a mighty hunter on earth with the beginning of his kingdom as Babel, Erech, Accad, and Calneh. A close examination of the Table of Nations passages seems to me that the Eurocentric scholars have missed the essential point and messages of the Table of Nations by suggesting that it is a comprehensive survey of international relations of the author to tell of the fulfillment of God's command to multiply and replenish.[15] The message and purpose of the Table of Nations is to teach the unity of mankind. The fact that all the people and nations of the world have one source and is one species, namely Homo Sapiens, is attested here.

Zephaniah and his Cushi Ancestry (Zeph. 1:1)

This is another occasion when Cush becomes a proper name, Cushi. The writer of the book of Zephaniah carefully traced the ancestry of Zephaniah to the fourth generation. In fact, not much is known about the background of this prophet, except his unusual extended genealogy. What is noteworthy here is the fact that seven of the Hebrew prophets (Amos, Obadiah, Micah, Nahum, Habakkuk, Haggai and Malachi) left their messages without their family history. It was just the father of six Hebrew prophets (Isaiah, Jeremiah, Hosea, Joel, Jonah and Ezekiel) that were named.[16] One of the benefits of this long genealogy is for readers to know that this prophet is a black man or has African Ancestry. Unfortunately, Eurocentric scholars have raised many objections to this interpretation with their usual attempt to de-Africanize the Bible. They have argued vehemently against this notion of African ancestry by saying that that section is a later addition; that the name *Cushi* is a common name in Ancient Near East and so does not imply African ancestry on the basis of chronology. They said that Zephaniah could not have any relation with Hezekiah, King of Judah. All these have no foundation if one honestly reflect on the history of African Diaspora, especially their interaction with the people of ancient Near East.[17] Israel in particular stayed in Africa for 430 years, most of the early generations of the Israel were born in Africa, married Africans, took African names, ate African food, and lived African life. During the eight-century, they were well known in ancient Israel. King Hezekiah depended upon

Africans to deliver Israel from the powerful Assyrians. The naked truth is that no king of ancient Israel interacted with Africans like that of Hezekiah. Since the genealogy of Zephaniah was traced to Hezekiah, king of Judah, the possibility is that he could have African ancestry.

The Reading of the Scroll by Cushi's Grandson, Yehudi (Jer. 36:1-23).

This passage deals with the reading of Jeremiah's scroll by a man called Jehudi, son of *Nethanyahu*, son of *Shelemayahu*, son of Cushi 36:14. Of all the princes present at this event, Yehudi, the grandson of *Cushi*, was the only person asked to read the scroll to the princes and later to King Jehoiakim. The possibility is that Yehudi was the only one who could read among the princes because the art of writing belonged to the professional during that period of the Bible. Another possibility is that, the content of the scroll was so disturbing that even the secretary had no courage to read it but Yehudi, the grandson of *Cushi* could if one remembers that the art of writing and reading took place in Africa (Egypt) long before any other ancient nation in the ancient Near East, Yehudi, the grandson of an African might have been taught how to write and read by his father or grandfather.

In the above account, there is a list of some important personalities involved, *Yehudi, ben Nethanyahu, ben Shelemeyahu, ben Cushi*(36:14, 21, 23). There are some unusual features about the personal identification of Yehudi that are worthy of discussion. It is unusual and remarkable that of all the princes present, only the ancestry of Yehudi was traced to the third generation, and to *Cushi*, which refers to black person of African descent. This was deliberately done for a purpose of revealing the African ancestry of Yehudi. However, some Eurocentric scholars who were feverishly trying to de-Africanize the Bible gave some untenable explanations of this unusual genealogy of Yehudi. Such scholars call for emendation of the text so that two personalities will be involved instead of

Cush as Africa in the Old Testament

one. It was suggested that the last *ben* which makes Yehudi to be the grandson of *Cushi* was originally a Hebrew conjunction *weeth* (and) instead of (*ben*-son).[18] Such emendation is questionable and has no basis except that it is based on scholastic prejudice. Eurocentric scholars think that since so much importance is attached to Yehudi, he could not had a grandfather who has an African ancestry.

Cush as a Geographic Reference

Six times the word Cush appears as a geographical location. In Genesis 2:13 river Gihon flows around the land of *Cush*. Genesis 2 described the Garden of Eden where Adam and Eve lived *originally*. There are four rivers in this garden, Pishon, Tigris and Euphrates and Gihon. Although scholars have no problem identifying rivers, Tigris, Euphrates, Pishon and Gihon have been problematic. Yet the location of these rivers leads to the correct location of the Garden of Eden. Pishon has been associated with canals such as Pallakopas in Mesopotamia, Phasis or Araxes Dowasir in Arabia, and even Indus and Ganges in India, by scholars. Gihon has also been associated with Oxus, Shatt en Nil, Khosper Mesopotamia and Rum in Arabia, and Nile in Africa. However, a close examination of the description of the last two rivers (Pishon and Gihon), helps to suggest the correct location of the rivers and the Garden of Eden. Pishon flows around the land of Havilah and is the land of gold, bdellim, and onyx stone. In another passages (I Chronicles 1:9, Gen. 10.7) Havilah was the son of *Cush*. The truth is that Africa has been recognized as the land famous for gold and minerals in antiquity. If Havilah is the son of Cush and Gihon surround the land of Cush, the most likely location of this river is Africa. The biblical records and the scientific discoveries that Africa is the origin of human race makes it possible that the Cush mentioned is the African Cush and not Mesopotamia as some Eurocentric scholars have attempted to de-Africanize the Bible.[19] In the book of

Esther 1:1 and 8:9, it appears as one of the two extreme boundaries of the Persian Empire which unquestionable locate *Cush* in Africa because Africa has earned the description of the far away country.

In Isaiah 18:1, *Cush* is referred to as the land that lies beyond Nile and send her ambassadors to the Nile river. Nile river is nowhere except in Africa. This is one of the places where Cush can be located in Africa with reasonable certainty. Despite the mention of river Nile, some scholars still maintain that this passage (Isaiah 18:1-6) refers to the Assyrians and not Africans. Others went as far as to conclude that it belong to the late post-exilic redactor. The description of the people of that nation as tall and smooth, the nation feared far and wide fits that of ancient African of that period. It was the period of the so-called Cushite Dynasty in Egypt that was so powerful to the extent that Hezekiah put his trust on them to deliver Judah from the terror of the Assyrians (Isaiah 20:1-6). The Prophet Isaiah vehemently opposed such dependence on African people (Egypt and Cush) instead of Yahweh. With the mention of Egypt, the location of Cush cannot be any other place but Africa.

Cush as Reference to People of African Descent.

The Cushit Wife of Moses (Num. 12:1)

The book of Numbers 12:1 recorded the incident of the challenge of Moses' leadership by Miriam when he (Moses) married a Cushit woman. Some Eurocentric scholars denied the passage above involving a cushit woman as authentic.[20] Scholars such as Ibn Ezra, J.J Owen, Elliot Binns, and Martin Noth identify the woman with Zipporah, the Midianite.[21] A close examination of the passages, shows that the Cushit woman was one of the nameless women in the Bible, but was identified by the color of her skin and ethnic origin. Comparison of this passage with other passages where the word *Cushi* and Cushit occur, shows

Cush as Africa in the Old Testament

that this woman cannot be a Midianite:

1. The passage does not make any attempt to associate the Cushite woman with Zipporah or a Midianite. It is dangerous to assume such by scholars.
2. That passage will not make sense if Cushit refers to Zipporah or a Midianite since Moses had married Zipporah forty (40) years before the Cushit woman because this event took place in the wilderness. Will it make sense for Miriam to get angry with Moses for the wife he had married forty years ago? Absolutely not. This must have been a new marriage, which took place in the wilderness probably after Zipporah had died or divorced Moses.
3. Midian and Zipporah were never referred to as *Cush* in any biblical record. Median and Cushite were never used interchangeably.
4. Moreover, the word, *Cush* in modern Hebrew means black. The original home of the black people is Africa.

If the word, *Cush* in modern Hebrew still means 'black' as it did in the ancient world, what would have been the most appropriate translation of the passage would be "a black woman or an African woman."

However, and very unfortunate indeed, most of the major translations chose to obscure the identity of that woman by transliterating it "Kushite woman." Some translators such as *King James Version* of 1611, *Douay Version* of 1609, and *The Contemporary English Version* of 1995 translate it "Ethiopian woman."[22] *Revised Standard Version* of 1952, *New Revised Standard Versions* of 1962, *The New English Bible* of 1976, *Berkely Version* of 1945, *American Standard Version* of 1901, *Jerusalem Bible* of 1966, and even *The Good News of* 1976 and *The Living Bibles* of 1971 transliterate it "a Kushite woman." The *Living Bible* adds a footnote that it refers to Zipporah the Midianite daughter of Reuel. Worst still *The Holy Bible* translated from the Latin Vulgate, of 1956, translates it "a desert woman." Eurocentric Biblical scholars knew that

"Behind every successful leader, there is a woman." To say, therefore, that an African woman contributed to the leadershipqualities of Moses appeared absurd to them, so they tried to de-Africanize the *Cushit*.

The Cushi Military man in King David's royal Army (II Sam. 18:21,31)

The majority of Eurocentric scholars have no problem identifying whom the *Cushi* was. They agree that he is of African descent. The problem is that since he is of African descent, he must be a slave, serving in David's army.[23] Others say that he is a mercenary from Africa. The truth is that, the Cushite could not be a slave because if he were a slave, he would have not been the one sent to the King. During a crisis at the battlefront, only a very high-ranking military officer would be sent to report such calamity to the king or president. The Eurocentric idea that the *Cushi* must be a slave or a mercenary does not make sense and is, therefore, untenable. It appears that the only reason they think he is of African descent is because he performs a function of being a messenger. It has no basis.

De-Africanization took place in many translations of the *English Bibles*. *English Bible* translated from the *Latin Vulgate* transliterated the name as *Cushi*, Duay version- *Cushai*, Berkley, King James, the Amplified Bible versions transliterated the passage as a proper name *Cushi*. But *the American Standard, Jerusalem Bible, the New Jerusalem Bible, the New English Bible*, Revised English Bible, transliterate it *Cushite* and a nameless person from the country of *Cush*. The Living Bible says, " a man from *Cush*," the *Contemporary English* version translates it "Ethiopian" with a footnote that Hebrew *Cush* refers to the region south of Egypt, part of present Ethiopia and Sudan. The most terrible translation is in the *Good News Bible*, which translates it "Sudanese slave."

Cush as Africa in the Old Testament

The Color of the Cushite (Jer. 13:23)

"Can Cushi change his skin or the leopard his spot? Then also you can do good who are customed to do evil!" is one of the proverbial saying in ancient Near East as part of the admiration of the black color of the Africans (cf. Isaiah 18:1-6 and 20:1-6). Unlike the Eurocentric scholars interpretation of this passage that the color of the skin of the Africans is despised by the Israelite, the passage is to express very vividly that there is a deep-seated wickedness in Judah which has been ingrained into the blood of the people for so many years that it has become permanent in the nature of the people of Judah. This is also a penetrating, pictorial portrayal of habit. If it is possible for Africans to change their color by washing, and leopard its color, then Judah would be able to change their evil habit that has become their nature. Most scholars have no problem identifying the Cushites here as Africans but feverishly interpreted the passage to mean that the ancient Near Eastern people despised the color of Africans.[24]

Ebed-Melech, the Cushi Delivered the Prophet Jeremiah (Jer. 38:7-13).

Eurocentric scholars do not have any problem identifying Ebed-Melech as having African ancestry, but his position in the court of Zedekiah is disputed. Ebed-Melech, the Cushite was also described as *saris*. Since the word *saris* could mean eunuch, Eurocentric scholars contended that Ebed-Melech must be a eunuch from Africa. This type of interpretation is based on racial prejudice of the interpreters. This word occurs about forty-five times in the Old Testament and in most cases do not mean eunuch since a eunuch is not permitted in the congregation of Israel. The truth is that the Hebrew word *saris* as used in the Old Testament could also mean "officer," "prince," "commander of the army," or "he who is at the head of the king," or "he who goes before the king, one of his confidential advisors."[25] Despite all these various meanings of the word *saris* in the Old Testament, these scholars prefer to see Ebed-Melech as a eunuch instead of the officer or adviser of the king since, to them nothing good comes from Africa. I maintain here that the word, *saris* here means officer or adviser.

The Translation of Cush in the Old Testament and the Implication for Church in Africa.

What I have done above is to trace some selective activities of the *Cush* and Cushites in the Old Testament and to highlight how some Eurocentric scholars have feverishly and consistently pursued the policy of de-Africanization of the Bible. The truth is that this policy also affects the translation of the Bible, especially the word, *Cush*. There have been so many inconsistencies in the translation of the word "*Cush*" in the Old Testament in the name of context as briefly discussed above. Peter Unseth, Knut Holter, and few other scholars have given a brief survey of the various translations of *Cush* in many versions of the Bible.[26] A close examination of various translations of *Cush* in various English Versions of the Bible shows that *Cush* was translated "Ethiopia", "Sudan," "Nubia", "desert wife." Other versions used the transliteration of *Cush* inconsistently with Ethiopia, Sudan and Nubia. I have suggested that the word *Cush/Cushite* should be translated Africa/ Africans. However these suggestions have been criticized by many colleagues, namely, Holter, Unseth, and Hoyland.[27] Marta Hoyland's article, "An African Presence in the Old Testament? David Tuesday Adamo's Interpretation of the Old Testament Cush Passages," seems to reveal her opinion about the presence of Africa and Africans in the Old Testament. Note the title with a question mark and her criticism of my work on *Cush*/Africa. She says:

> By analyzing the texts he wants to elevate the African people and the African continent to the position he claims they had in ancient times..........However, Adamo's approach has also weak sides. One is that he becomes one-sided. In my work with Adamo's analysis of the Cush passages in the OT, I find that he always finishes with the same set of conclusion. It seems as if Adamo approaches the texts predisposed. He finds what he searches for, even though the texts vary with regard to both form and content. In his eagerness to put Africa and Africans to the fore, he exaggerates, giving no room for exegetical discussions, because he concludes before he asks. This approach of Adamo makes his analysis predictable an superficial, as it prevents him from approaching each text with different questions. It also makes the reader feel suspicious, and one asks whether Adamo treats the passages with sufficient exegetical respect.[28]

Hoyland's comment above reminds me of a time I sent one of my articles on *Cush* to an editor of a journal and one of the assessors said, "the author of this article is trying to smuggle Africa into the Bible." Any objective Old Testament researcher should know that I am not trying to smuggle or to elevate Africa in the Bible. The honest truth is that the people of ancient Israel had acknowledged and elevated them. The Bible is consistent about Africans. They were mentioned in every strand of biblical literature. Ancient Israel trusted them and depended on them. God made it possible for Africa and Africans to participate in the biblical drama of redemption. The only problem is that the Eurocentric scholars who consistently dominated the translation and interpretation of the Bible did not want to bring it out to the open. What I am trying to do is trying to reveal what is already there in the Bible. Except Hoyland wants to deny the fact that *Cush* in the Bible referred to Africa and Africans, by ignoring so many passages that persistently made it clear that *Cush*/Cushite points to the direction of Africa as Holter has acknowledged, "...that Old Testament translators should inform their readers, in footnotes or glossary entries that Cush in most cases refers to an African nation that is well attested also in extra-biblical sources."[29] Peter Unseth is also clear about this, "..I think that the list shows that there is clearly a significant Black African presence in the Old Testament, and that Israel and the Middle East had much awareness of and contact with Black Africa."[30] Could Hoyland's further comments on my exegetical suspicion be a typical Eurocentric scholar's way of suspecting anything good that comes from Africa?

Although Dr. Holter agrees with the presence of Africa and Africans in the Old Testament, he opposes the translation of Cush/Cushite to Africa and Africans. He prefers the transliteration of the word *Cush*. His main reasons are the possibility of translation problem and endless debate of whether all references to Cush in the Old Testament refer to Africa, and the ideological connotations both politically and theologically. If the majority of references to Cush refer to Africa (where we have a clear identification), this problem of endless debate should not even come up. Other references that are not clear cut should equally be translated Africa because there is no single clear-cut evidence that such reference to Cush refers to Mesopotamia, Arabia, or India, which the majority of Eurocentric scholars suggested. Ideological problems have no basis for not translating *Cush* as Africa. The truth is that Biblical scholars are the ones concerned with such ideologies when reading the Bible. Ordinary readers, who are the majority of readers of the Bible, do not really care about such ideologies. The suggestion by Holter to transliterate all references to *Cush* with addition of footnotes is unacceptable. Again the majority of ordinary readers are not concerned with reading footnotes. Real committed ones do not believe in footnotes, but the very word of God in the Bible. More seriously, the transliteration still conceals the African identity with reference to *Cush*. That is also the major strategic attempt of Eurocentric scholars to conceal African identity and their participation in the drama of redemption. Ordinary readers (especially those in Africa) just do not know what

Cush as Africa in the Old Testament

Cush means in the Bible. The hermeneutical problem of transferring the idea of Africans being enemies of the chosen people is not a sufficient reason for hiding the African identity in the Bible. The Cush passages where these negative ideas came up are very few and can be understood in their context by the ordinary readers.

As Unseth has maintained, the translation of Cush into any single modern state in Africa, such as Ethiopia or Sudan, is misleading because it does not adequately represent the extent of the land of the black people referred to in the Bible. I understand that it is impossible to have a perfet translation. However, what we need to do is to seek the most accurate translation which does not conceal the presence of Africa and Africans in the Bible. We should seek the translation that will be understood by the ordinary readers. I, therefore hold firmly to my previous suggestion that where *Cush* refers to a geographical location, it should be translated *Africa*. Where is refers to name of people, *Africans* or *Black African man* or *woman*. In Africa, it is not unusual for certain persons to bear the names of their towns, districts, and countries. Moreover, the Alexandrian (LXX) translators had done this by translating *Cush* to Ethiopia, which was perfectly accurate then.[31] The translation of the word *Mitzrayim* to Egypt in English versions is another example. If that Hebrew word can be translated to Egypt in English versions, there is no reason why *Cush* cannot be translated to Africa. Another example is the word, which is, translated Assyria in the biblical text. Again, if that Hebrew word could be translated Assyria why do my critics take exception to Africa knowing that Egypt and Ethiopia are within the geographical location of Africa.

Another reason and advantage of translating Ethiopia to Africa and Africans is that, there is no continent in world whose achievements have been misunderstood, misrepresented and whose glory has given to other nations like the continent of Africa. It seems to me that the agitation to continued to transliterate the

Hebrew words *cush* is part of the continue attempt or conspiracy to obscure the achievement of Africans and given to other nations.

If Cush is translated as I have suggested above, the implication is great. Africa and Africans will know that Yahweh has also done great things through their ancestors. It destroys the satanic ideology that Christianity is a foreign religion. It also disproves the racist idea that some Eurocentric scholars have forced into the Bible. It can further affect the growth of Christianity in Africa.

I still hold tenaciously to my position that the present English translation of the Bible that is in circulation is a disservice to Africans and African Diaspora all over the world. The identity of the black people that is in the Bible is[32] concealed. There is a difference between footnotes and the real biblical text. I look forward to the day when a committee of African translators will come out boldly to retranslate correctly the text in the Bible to reflect the presence of Africa and Africans in the Bible. I believe that there will be a new awakening in Africa and among the black people all over the world.

Cush as Africa in the Old Testament

Endnotes

[1] This article was presented at the conference on Africa in the Old Testament, Nairobi, 1999 . A different version of this essay was later published under the title " Images of Cush in the Old Testament,"by Peter Lang Publishing, New York, 2000.
[2] Originally published by Christian Universities Press (San Francisco: 1998) and reprinted by Wipf and Stock Publishers, Oregon, USA, 2000.
[3] Gaston Maspero, *The Dawn of Civilization* vol. I. Trans. by M. L Mclure (New York: Frederick Ungar Publication Co. Reprinted 1968), 488.
[4] J. H Breasted, *Ancient Records of Egypt*, vol.1 (Chicago: University of Chicago Press, 1906), 251.
[5] D.T. Adamo, *Africa and Africans in the Old Testament*, 11.

[6] Ibid.
[7] Ibid.
[8] Ibid.,See pages 11-13.
[9] *Ancient Near Eastern Text Relating to the Old Testament* (Princeton: Princeton University Press, 1969), 292.
[10] Ibid., 293. See also Daniel David Luckenbill, *Ancient Records of Assyria and Babylon*(New York: Greenwood Press, 1968), Vol. 2, 285.
[11] Ibid.
[12] Ibid.,
[13] E.A Wallis Budge, *The Egyptian Sudan*, vol. 2, 415-16.
[14] The Hebrews, the Assyrians and the Babylonians, the Greeks see them as such. That is why some times the mentioned them together most of the time.
[15] von Rad, *Genesis*. Revised edition, Translated by J.H Marks, (Philadelphia: Westminster Press, 1972),143.
[16] Adamo, *Africa and the Africans in the Old Testament*, 116119.
[17] Ibid., See also Ronoko Rashidi, "African Presence in Asia," in *Nile Valley Civilization*, edited by Ivan Van Sertima,(New Brunswick Transaction Periodical Consortium, 1985).
[18] See the discussion in *Africa and the Africans* for the list of these scholars, 110-111.
[19] See *Africa and the Africans*, 56-57 for the list of these scholars who have attempted to de-Africanize the Bible.
[20] W. Coats, Martin Noth, V.Fritz and W. Rudolph are among the Eurocentric scholars who treat such passage as supplementary. For a summary of the discussion, see *Africa and Africans in the Old Testament*, 67-69.
[21] See Adamo, *Africa and Africans in the Old Testament*, 69
[22] That is still not appropriate because no one knows from which part of Africa the black woman came from. It could be Egypt, Congo, South Africa, Kenya, or even Nigeria.
[23] William Mckane, *I & II Samuel* (London: SCM Press,1963), 37-60; Peter R. Ackroyd, *The Second Book of Samuel* (Cambridge: Cambridge University Press, 1977), 172; Ben F Philbeck, Jr., *The Broadman Bible Commentary I Samuel-Nehemiah*, edited by C.J. Allen, Vol. 3, (Nashville:

Broadman Press, 1970), 129; Edward Ullendorf, *Ethiopia and the Bible* (Oxford: OUP.,1968), Charles Copher, "Egypt and Ethiopia in the Old Testament," in the *Nile Valley Civilizations* (New Brunswick: Transation Periodical Consortium, 1985), 173; Henry Smith, *The Books of Samuel: International Crititical Commentary* (Edinburgh: T & T Clark, 1910), 359.

24Ibid.,109.

25ibid., 114-115.

26Knut Holter, "Old Testament 'Cush' as 'Africa'. *The Bible Translator*, Technical Papers Vol.48.No 3 (July 1997), 331-336; Peter Unseth, "Hebrew Cush: Sudan, Ethiopia, or Where?" Unpublished article, 1999. I must appreciate Rev. McKissic for calling my attention to this paper.

27Ibid., Marta Hoyland, "An African Presence in the Old Testament? David Tuesday Adamo's Interpretation of the Old Testament Cush Passages," *Old Testament Essays* 11/1 (1998), 50-58.

28*Old Testament Essays*, 11/1 (1998), 50-58.

29Should Old Testament 'Cush' be rendered 'Africa'."? 336.

30Peter Unseth," Hebrew Cush:Sudan, Ethiopia, or Where?" Unpublished article, 1990, 11.

31Adamo, *Africa and the Africans*, 28-37.

GENESIS CREATION ACCOUNT IN AFRICAN BACKGROUND[1]

Introduction

For the ancient Israelites, the idea that God is the creator is not disputed. It is presupposed and affirmed in their thought. In their thought there could have been no other way in which the heaven and the earth have originated. Therefore we see in Genesis that 'In the beginning God created the heavens and the earth' (1:1). This idea of creation runs throughout the entire Old Testament. It was retold and contextualized over again. To emphasize the repetition of the idea of creation throughout the entire Bible, Martin Luther said that 'he who would understand the first chapter of Genesis needs to have studied and digested all sacred scriptures.[2] [3]Although creation faith holds a less important place in the Old Testament concept than salvation and election, the Christian Church stood firmly with the biblical account of creation (with the affirmation in her creed 'creator of heaven and earth') until the rise of natural sciences during the age of the enlightenment, which brought serious opposition to the biblical ecclesiastical tradition.

Like the ancient Israelites, practically all Africans consider God as the creator of the world. Even in this technological age, it is beyond the imagination of an ordinary African who has not been brainwashed by the mentality of the West to consider any other way in which the world could have been created. This belief in God as the creator makes this one of the commonest attributes of God among Africans and is expressed in their different versions of myths, names given to God, prayers and praises.[4]

This chapter is an attempt to understand the Genesis creation accounts in African context. This I hope to accomplish by a comparative study of the Genesis and African creation accounts, and the implication of the similarities and differences.

Genesis and African Creation Myths

One of the most common ways of affirming God as the creator in Africa is by calling him various names. These names picture God as a carver, maker, originator, inventor, builder and others. Apart from these names, myths are also a very strong vehicle by which Africans affirm their faith in God as the creator of the heaven and the earth. These myths are in different versions from one place to another and are contradictory a times. However, most of the time they have common motifs, common theology and common elements. Since the Genesis creation myth is indeed a very popular one, which I believe most of my readers are well acquainted with, I will not waste time describing the Genesis account, but rather, some of the African creation myths which may not be well known to some of my readers.

The creation myth of the Yoruba of Nigeria has two versions.[5] After the earth has been created in four days, the fifth day was a day of rest and worship. The Supreme God (*Olodumare*) sent his deputy (*Orisanla*), accompanied by a counsellor (*Orunmila*),[6] to 'embellish' the earth. He was given a primeval palm tree, silk rubber tree, white wood, and *dodo* to plant so that their seeds would be for drink and food. After *Orisanla* had completed his job, Olodumare sent *Oreluere*, who led a party of beings to the earth. *Orisanla* was also assigned another job: molding human being from the dust of the earth in physical forms, but *Olodumare* alone was to give life.

Another version of the Yoruba creation myth says that the task given to *Orisanla*, who was his deputy, was later accomplished by another agent of *Olodumare, Oduduwa*. This happened because *Orisanla* was drunk with palm wine and fell asleep on the way to the earth. God then reassigned his job to *Oduduwa*, who performed the task of planting the trees and molding man's physical being.

According to the creation myth of the Vugusa people of Kenya,[7] after God had created the heavens (in two days) he created his dwelling place and that of his two assistants. He also created the moon, the sun, the stars, rain, rainbows, and then the earth with mountains and valleys for his two assistants. Then God created man and woman. Lastly he created plants, animals, birds and other creatures. After all of these were completed in six days, he rested on the seventh day because it was a bad day.

The Ashanti creation myth of Ghana says that after God had created the sky, the earth, rivers, waters, plants and tree, then he created man. He also made animals for man's use. God later made the spirits of the mountains, forest, and rocks to protect man.[8]

According to the Bambuti[9] of the Congo, the heaven above and the earth below were God's home until dust began to fall and God feared that his food might be contaminated. He then ordered the lightning to find him another abode above the earth. He did, in heaven, by dividing the earth from the above. God and moon, his closest being, went upward to dwell. Then he created the chameleon, water, trees, mankind (but woman first) and then animals, the 'celestial goat' being the ancestor of all animals.

The Azande[10] of Sudan creation myths have many versions. The most prominent says that God put all the creatures in a sealed canoe leaving only a waxed hole on it. Then he set his sons, moon, sun, night, cold and stars — on the task of opening the canoe to discover what was inside the canoe. The sun opened the canoe by heating it, because God's messenger had revealed the secret to him. Then all animals, rivers, trees, hills and grass came out.

The Fon people[11] of Dahomey say that sometime, somewhere, Da, God's assistant appeared. Sometimes he is called the first created being, which set up four pillars to sustain the sky and caused his excreta to form waterways on earth. God, however, created vegetation, animals and later mankind from the clay and water. He also created the divinities as his children and set the entire universe in order.

Comparison of Biblical and African Creation Myths

Difference

In African creation myths, almost all versions say that God had an assistant who helped him in the work of creation. These are the divinities. The Yoruba version called the assistant *Obatala* or *Oduduwa*. The Fon call him *Da*. However, in Genesis God alone created not only the heaven and the earth, but also all that are in them. In Genesis we have the record of all God's activities. 'In the beginning God created the heaven and the earth' (1: 1). 'God's Spirit moved upon the face of the waters'. God himself created the light (1: 3—4), the firmament (1: 9—10), the grass (1: 11—12), and all the creatures, both animal and man (1: 20—31).

In the African myths, there is no idea of chaos or the deep when God created the heaven and the earth. However, Genesis 1: 2 says: "And the earth was without form, and void; and darkness was upon the face of the deep and the spirit of God moved upon the face of the waters" (KJV). According to the African creation myths known to us so far, there is no idea of mankind created in the image of God as it is in the biblical account in Genesis 1: 26. This is a very remarkable difference between the African and biblical creation myths, because this enabled mankind to be the apex of creation and to be able to have fellowship with God. Genesis 1: 26—27 says:

Genesis Creation Account in African Background

> And God said, Let us make man in our image, after our likeness: and let them have dominion over the flesh of the sea, and over the fowl of the air, and over the cattle, and over all the earth, and over every creeping thing that creepeth upon the earth. So God created man in his own image, in the image of God created he him; male and female created he them.

As mentioned previously, while the seventh day of the rest is an evil day in African myth (Vugusu of Kenya), it is a holy day in the biblical myth:

> And on the seventh day God ended his work, which he had made; and he rested on the seventh day from all his work, which he had made. And God blessed the seventh day and sanctified it because that in it he had rested from all his work, which God created (Genesis 2: 2—3).

In the creation account of the African people, the moon, and the trees are personified. According to the Azande of Sudan, God set his sons —moon, sun, stars and others — the task of opening the sealed canoe where he put all the creatures. However, nowhere in Genesis is an inanimate object personified and participated in the work of creation.

Finally, the African creation myths are polytheistic. There is always the account of the divinities present. But the biblical account is monotheistic, as far as the Genesis account is concerned.

Similarities

As there are differences between the Genesis and African accounts of creation, so also are there some fundamental similarities that must not be ignored, because there are reasons for these similarities.

In both the African and the biblical creation accounts, God is regarded as the creator and the controller of the universe. According to the Yoruba, Vugusu, Ashanti,

Bambuti and the Azande, as discussed previously, the supreme God is the creator of the heaven and the earth. This fact is not questioned or disputed. Although there might be some assistants who continued to create things on the earth, yet basically God is the creator of the heaven and the earth and gives instruction to those divinities, in the case of the Yoruba and Fon myths in Nigeria and Dahomey, respectively.

In the order of creation, in both in African and the biblical accounts, the heaven and the earth are the first things to be created by God (Genesis 1: 1). Then, the rest of the inhabitant of the heaven and the earth were created in an ongoing process of creation.

In almost all the versions of African accounts, the creation of mankind involved the creation of male and female, as in Genesis 1: 27: 'so God created man in his own image, in the image of God created he him; male and female created he them' (K.JV). However, in some cases (e.g., Vugusu, Bambuti) man was not the first to be created. The Bambuti believe that woman was created before man.

In some African accounts of creation, the creation of man from the dust or clay of the earth is mentioned, as it in Genesis 2: 7: "And the Lord God formed man of the dust of the ground and breathed into his nostril the breath of life; and man became a living soul." (KJV)

However, in the case of the Yoruba people of Nigeria, one version indicates that *Obatala*, God's deputy, was in charge of molding human beings, but God has the right and power of giving life to the molded mankind. In both the African and biblical accounts of creation mankind was given power over all the rest of creation, as in Genesis 1: 26:

> And God said, let us make man in our image, after our likeness; and let them have dominion over the fish of the sea, and over the fowl of the air, and over the cattle, and over all the earth, and over every creeping thing that creepeth upon the earth. (KJV).

Genesis Creation Account in African Background

The idea of God resting on the seventh day was present in both the African and the biblical ideas of creation. However, while that of seventh day in Genesis 2: 2—3 was a holy day because it was 'sanctified and blessed by God', according to the Vugusu myths God rested on the seventh day because it was a bad day.

The idea of the fall of mankind is present in both creation myths. According to one version of the Yoruba myth, *Obatala* got drunk on his way to the earth and therefore could not perform the work of creation assigned to him. God chose *Oduduwa* to perform the work. The Bambuti of Ghana believe that God inhabited the earth and the heaven until dust began to fall and God feared contamination of his food. So he went far upward to dwell. Genesis describes the Biblical account of the fall. Another version of the Yoruba myth says that the sky, God's abode, was originally closer to the earth than this, until a woman who was pounding yam hit the sky with her mortar and God moved his abode (sky) upward far from the earth.

Finally, one of the most important similarities is in their theological concepts. In the biblical account, Israel had to first of all experience God's greatness in delivering his people from bondage, his preservation and his making them a great nation before they could fully realize God's creative power, greatness and lordship.[12] After all these experiences, Israel could then affirm clearly in the Genesis account of creation that Yahweh who has redeemed us is the creator and the Lord of all that is. Both P and J express this affirmation.

A look at various African creation accounts has revealed this same affirmation. According to the Yoruba people, *Olodumare* is always in control. He gives order to all the divinities that did not act in isolation. That is why they called him *Oluwa* (Lord) and *Olorun* (the owner of heaven). According to the Azande, God put all the world's creatures in a canoe; the Bambuti see the heaven and the earth as God's throne. The Lugbara see God as 'the ultimate fountain head of all power and authority'.[13]

Another theological affirmation of both the Genesis

and African creation myths is the transcendence and the immanence of God. In the Genesis account, his transcendence is stressed by His creation by word, that is, the primacy of His will and the ease of His work. His immanence is stressed in His breath into man, which suggests His intimate involvement in creation. That also becomes the basis for His intimate relationship and communion with His creation. In African myths, God's transcendence is affirmed not only in the ease with which He created the heaven and the earth but also in His abode in heaven and the order He gives to the divinities that were His assistants who duly carry out his order on earth. His breath of life affirms his immanence that He only has the right to give (according to the Yoruba account).

The Genesis account also stressed the omnipotence of God. Both *P* and *J* consider his ability to create out of nothing *(creatio ex nihilo)* as an expression of his omnipotence. This *creatio ex nihilo* is also expressed among the Banyarwanda of Rwanda: God created the world out of nothing.[14] Both the African and the Genesis creation myths affirm that absolute power belongs to God, the source of everything that exists.

God as creator of the world in both the African and Genesis creation accounts means that he encompass the complete time process, ruling, determining and completing all ages.

Implications

The comparative study of the Genesis and African myths has some implications, which will be discussed, in this section. After a comparative study of the Genesis and the Mesopotamian creation story, the most common conclusion by Eurocentric biblical scholar is that the source of the Genesis creation account is Mesopotamia, without regard to the possibility of other sources. E.A. Speiser, on the basis of linguistic similarity between the Mesopotamian and the Genesis creation accounts; G.W. Coats, in his discussion of the literary forms of the Genesis creation account; and Claus Westermann, J.L. McKenzie and Morris Jastrow, on the basis of recurring motifs in both accounts, conclude that the source of the story is Mesopotamia.[15]

However, it is time for a further examination of other accounts for a possible ultimate source of the Genesis creation account other than Mesopotamia. The few African myths that have been discussed previously show that Africans have abundant myths similar to that of the Mesopotamian and Israelite. In the light of the similarities in content, motifs and theology there is the possibility of contact.

There are several suggested possibilities of how the Hebrew came in contact with the creation myths of Africa. The first possibility was during their sojourn in Egypt. They lived in Africa for about 430 years (Exodus 12: 44). During this period, they probably learnt the myths but did not take them very seriously until they came across a similar Mesapotamian myth, which threatened their faith. They were then forced to re-examine their faith in terms of the African and Mesopotamian version of the myth. The second possibility is that the Mesopotamians had trade contact as early as the third millennium BC. According to the inscriptions of Sargon of Agade and Gudea of Lagash, the main source of trade between the Mesopotamians and the Africans — called Magan (Egypt) and Melluhhan (Ethiopia) was 'gold in dust form', logs, ivory and others.[16] What probably happened was that the Sumerians perfected and localized the African myths. The Israelites then came in contact with these myths, which threatened their faith in Yahweh. It was probably not until the period of the exile that they were able to contextualize the myths in the light of their faith in Yahweh.

The third possibility is that both Sumerians and Israelite came in contact with these myths in Africa, but Israel did not take it very seriously until they came in contact with the Sumerian version of the African myth in Canaan, which threatened their faith in Yahweh.

Genesis Creation Account in African Background

One may then ask what is responsible for the differences. The reason for the difference could be that the nature of a floating oral tradition, when such a story is repeatedly told and diffused in different places, it usually loses its original proper names and local color. It is therefore, possible that the creation myths ultimately originated from Africa and, by the time they reached the Sumerians and Israel it had lost its proper names and local color, while still retaining its essential motifs and theology.

Endnotes

[1] This article was formerly published in *Caribbean Journal of Religious Studies*, vol. 10, no 2 (Sept. 1989), 17-25

[2] J.D. Smart, *The Old Testament in Dialogue with Modern Man* (Philadelphia: The Westminster Press, 1952), 2—5.

[4] J.S. Mbiti, *Concepts of God in Africa* (London: S.P.C.K., 1970), 49.

[5] E.B. Idowu, *Olodumare: God in Yoruba Belief* (London: Longmans, 1962), 18—22.

[6] *Orunmila* was the only being who knew the secret of giving life because he was with Olodumare from the beginning. He also knew the secret of the existence of all the divinities because he was endowed with unique wisdom and foreknowledge, That is the reason he was able to be a counsellor of *Orisanla*.

[7] J.S. M.biti, *Concepts of God in Africa*, 48.

[8] Ibid. *op. cit.*,49

[9] P. Shebesta, *Revisiting My Pigmy Host* (London: E.T., 1936), 168-169.

[10] J.S. Mbiti, *Concepts of God in Africa, op. cit.*, 49.

[11] Ibid., *op. cit.*, 50.

[12] W. Dryness, *Themes in Old Testament Theology* (Downer Grove: Intervarsity Press, 1979)64.

[13] J.S. Mbiti, *Concepts of God in Africa, op. cit.*, 51.

[14] Ibid., 50

[15] E. A. Speiser, *Genesis — The Anchor Bible*, 3rd ed. (Garden City, N.Y:Doubleday and Co., 1979). Coats, *Genesis*, Vol.1, translated by William Heynen (Grand Rapids: W.B. Erdmans Publishing Company, 1983). Westermann, *Genesis 1—11,* Translated by J.J. (Minneapolis:

Augsburg Publishing House, 1984), 212—213. J.L. McKenzie, 'The literary characteristic of Genesis 2—3', *Theological Studies*, 15 *(1954)*, 491—572 Jastrow, *Religion of Babylonia and Assyria* (New York: Charles Scribner's Sons, 1914), 5—7.

[16]Some scholars argue that Magan and Meluhhan cannot be Egypt and Ethiopia, respectively. However, C.J. Gad, Sir Henry Rawlinson and Noah Kramer maintain that Magan and Meluhhan should be located in Africa Gad, 'The Invasion of Agade and the Gutian Invasion', *Cambridge Ancient Histo,y*, Vol. 1 (Cambridge: Cambridge University Press, 1981), Part 2A, . 453-54. Rawlinson, *History of Herodotus*, Book I, translatedby Professor Rawlinson, with Essay VI in its Appendix. Kramer, *The Sumerians* (Chicago: University of Chicago Press, 1970), 61.

DEUTERONOMIC CONCEPTION OF GOD AND ITS IMPORTANCE IN AFRICAN CONTEXT (DEUT. 6:4)[1]

Introduction

Although the book of Deuteronomy has received some considerable attention among scholars, there has been no unanimous agreement among theses scholars as to its dating, authorship, central theology, its relationship to the Josiah's law of 622 BCE. The translation itself constitutes a problem. A brief consideration shall be given to these critical problems as a background to this essay. But the purpose of this writing is not a detail rehearsal of the above critical history of research. The main purpose is the examination of Deuteronomic conception of God according to Deuteronomy 6:4 and its importance in African context. This examination shall include its translation, the nature of SEMA passages, its central theme and the importance of this conception to African Christianity.

Translation

The English word, "Deuteronomy" is a transliteration of the Greek and Latin words, *Deuteronomion* and

Deuteronomium respectively. The Greek, as well as Latin words, simply means "repetition." This follows the LXX rendering of the Hebrew expression *Misheneh*, which means " the copy of the Law" in Deuteronomy 17:18. This Greek and Latin renderings are misleading for several reasons. First, this title is a misinterpretation of Deuteronomy 17:18. Second, it does not represent any of the original titles of the Hebrew Bible given to it by the Jews. These titles are *ele wadbarim* ("these are the words") *debarim* (words) or *Mishneh Hathorah* (copy of the law) or *shepher* to *khahoth* (the book of admonitions).

The importance of discussing this title is that all the translators of the title of Deteronomy into all the three major Nigerian languages (Yoruba, Hausa, Ibo and others) followed the above misleading title. The Yoruba translators transliterated it to *Deuteronomi* instead of translating the Hebrew title *debarim* to *Awon Oro*. The Hausa translators translated it to *kubawa sharia* instead of *Li tafi Sharia*. The Ibo translators transliterated Deuteroomy to *Deuteronomi* like the Yoruba language instead of *Iwu*. Unfortunately the translators of the three main Nigerian languages transliterated the entire Pentateuchal books.[2]

As there exists a problem in the translation of the title of the book, so also exists a problem with the translation of the *SEMA* passage (*sema Yisrael YHWH Elohenu YHWH Ehad* Dut. 6:4). The nature of the Hebrew is enigmatic. This is true when one considers several possible translation of the verse. RSV. KJV., and the New World Translation are in one accord: "Here O Israel: The Lord our God is one LORD" (Deut. 6:41). The nature of the Hebrew name is enigmatic. This is true when one considers several possible translations of the Verse. *RSV, KJV.* and *The New World Translation* are in one accord: "Here O Israel: The Lord our God- is one LORD."[3] *The Jerusalem Bible* translates, "Listen, Israel: Yahweh our God is the one Yahweh." It introduces 'an additional definite article "the". *The New American Standard Bible* -Translates: "Hear, O, Israel the LORD is our God, the LORD is One."' This translation adds two verbs to be. The NIV. reads:

"Hear O Israel, the LORD is our God, is One." It also has an additional footnote agreeing with RSV. KJV., Jerusalem, and *The New American 'Standard Bible*. In the same footnote, it suggests another translation, "The LORD is our God, the LORD alone." C. F. Keil and F. Delitssch condemn this translation with "Yahweh alone',' as suggested by the footnote of the NIV because the Hebrew word, is not Yahweh *lebado*. It appears that there is no unanimous agreement as to the exact translation of Deuteronomy 6:4. This type of problem also exists among scholars when the content of the entire book is examined critically.

Critical Problem of the Book of Deuteronomy

As discussed earlier in my introduction, the discussion of the historical critical problem will be brief and will be given only as a background of this article. The major, critical problem of the book of Deuteronomy can be divided into two-dating and analysis of Deuteronomy. The problem of dating and authorship begins with the recognition of some Church Fathers (Athanasius, Jerome, Procoplus of Gara, and Chrysostom) who related the content of the book of Deuteronomy to Josiah's reform programmed in 621 BCE. (II Kgs. 22f). However, the actual critical presentation was made by W.M.L. de wette who was generally accepted by scholars (although with some variations), and it became significant for the understanding of Deuteronomy and the Pentateuch as a whole.[4] 'While scholars like Holscher[5] argue for an exilic or postexilic origin :of Deuteronomy, J. Lindblom and Weindfeld consider it as the compilation by scribe or priests beginning from the seventh century BCE.[6] However, D.W.B. Rebinson, ascribes it to Moses.[7] Many scholars consider the problem of analysis of Deuteronomy crucial. Although there are large measures of agreement that there is a relationship between the law book found in the temple in 622/621-BCE, and that this, law book is preserved in Deuteronomy, there are wide disagreement on how to separate the original Deuteronomy, the law book itself, from our book of Deuteronomy. It is also widely agreed upon that the law of Josiah is not identical with the book of Deuteronomy. There is also a question of the appearance of duplications 'and, unevenness of various kinds to be found in the beginning and the end (1-11 and 27-34), and the central section of Deuteronomy (12-26), which contains the actual laws.

Several attempts to provide a solution to the above' problems may be divided into two main groups. The first group assumes that the book of Deuteronomy is a product of successful amplifications" of Josianic law book. Scholars like F. Horst, J. Hempel," Holscher are representatives of this first idea.[8] Horst tried to prove the existence of an older Pre-Deuteronomic basis for Deuteronomy 12-18 which he said had gone through a threefold elaboration and supplementation.[9] The second group described the present book of Deuteronomy as a product of the combination of two or more editions of the original Deuteronomy. The representative of this group are scholars like Stevernagel and Wellhausen.[10] Wellhausen, in his study' of Deuteronomy, sees a combination of two editions in chapters 12-26. He therefore allocated chapters 1-4 (Introduction), 27 (conclusion) to the edition of 12-26, and chapters 5-11 as introduction, and 28-30 as a conclusion to another edition of chapters 12-26. However, Martin Noth's opinion appears to be more influential. He sees chapters 1-3 (4) as an introduction to the Deuteronomistic work (Joshua, Samuel and Kings) while chapters 5-11 may be considered as an introduction to the actual Deuteronomic Law.

Another critical approach to the book of Deuteronomy is the form critical and traditio-critical analysis. Accepting Klosterman's idea, von Rad sees Deuteronomy as a reflection of "a history of a paraenotic use of the law, which has its setting in the "ancient Israelite cult of amphhictyony.[11] G. Mandenhall examining the parallel between the Hittite suzerain treaties and the legal tradition of the Pentateuch concluded that the book of Deuteronomy was influenced by the Hittite Suzerain ' treaties.[12] One of the recent traditio-critical theories is the idea that Deuteronomy is a composition of the sages and scribes from the royal house of Judah in the seventh to eighth centuries BCE. The book of Deuteronomy, he says, is a reflection of the ancient Near Eastern Wisdom.[13]

The Nature and Importance of *SEMA* (Deut. 6:4)

In the analysis of the book of Deuteronomy, which I have discussed previously, the tendency by scholars is to regard the *SEMA* passage (Deut. 6:4) as not being essentially part of the original or nucleus of the book of Deuteronomy. This passage is considered a mere introduction to Deuteronomy 12-26, which is considered the nucleus or the original passage. Despite the problem of the English translation and the unsolved critical analysis of the book, yet the essential meaning and the importance of the *SEMA* passage are clear- that of the part of the exposition of the Commandments or Mosaic laws. The passage is a summary or the conclusion of the Old Testament understanding of God as monotheistic according to Israel's experience of God's activities in their history. It is a proclamation of God's Oneness, Uniqueness, and Jealousy. Despite 'the critical problem and the ambiguous translation, the text is still regarded as one of the most important and precious text in the Old Testament Scriptures.

There is no evidence of omission or corruption of the passage in any of the MSS available to scholars so far. To Jesus Christ, Deuteronomy 6:4-5 is the first and the greatest commandment. This text is so important that it is recorded in all the synoptic Gospels (Mark 12:28-34; Matt. 22:34-40; Luke 10: 25-28). This text is unique in the entire Old Testament. It does not have any parallel in the Pentateuch especially, when one considers the way it combines the commandment in term of absolute love with the expression of the unity, singleness and uniqueness of God. To the Jews, the words of the SEMA are even higher than the words of the Decalogue (Deut. 6:4). As the words

"There is no God but Allah is the first pillar of Islamic faith, so also is the *SEMA* the symbol of the Jewish faith. It opens the Jewish synagogue and is recited twice everyday. It is also recited every Friday and Saturday as the Torah is taken *out* Of the ark to be read.[14] It is written in the parchment, worn in the phyilatery, and written on the doorposts by the Jews.[15]

The Oneness and Uniqueness of *YHWH*

A close examination of Deut. 6:4 reveals that in a verse of only six words, the designation of God as *YHWH* occurs twice. This Deuteronomic designation of God as *YHWH*, especially as YHWH *ehad* in Deut. 16.14 definitely has some significance. Perhaps, that is why Deuteronomy has a characteristic focus in the "name theology" and very concerned with causing the name of *YHWH* to dwell among his people. However, for us to grasp that significance is it important to disuses very briefly the meaning of the word *YHWH*. The word *YHWH* has short forms *(YH, WHH, YHW)*. It appears that the origin of the name goes back beyond the period of Moses, like the other component forms (*Yau or Yau'm*) which are also found in Babylonian names of the third Millenium *Lipusyam, Yaubani*.[16]

This Tetragrammaton as a personal name occurs 5,321 times in the Old Testament. The use of this divine name goes back to the earliest time in Genesis 4:1, 26; 9:26, Exodus 6:3 where the Lord reveals to Moses what His name is. When Moses asked for God's name God said to him, "I will be what I 'Will be," that is, in Hebrew *eheye asher eheye*. The origin of the personal name seems to have been from the verb to be *Hawa:* According to Exodus 3:14 it represents the simple Qal, imperfect YHWH. YHWH then seems to mean "He is; He exists, and actively present. According to Eichrodt, the emphasis is not passive but active existence.[17] Although the use of YHWH in Deut. 6:4 also means all that the name means throughout the Old Testament, that is, the active existence, the fact of his immediate nearness and concrete presence (Ex. 62, 4,

Deut. 7:9), his love, and concern, for Israel in revealing his redemptive covenant, the one, who cause to be," or create"[18] his immutability (Ex. 3:15), God as a judge and 'warrior. (*YHWH Sabaoth*), and his holiness, his most significant emphasis is *YHWH*'s oneness and Uniqueness. Just as Isaiah of Jerusalem recognized the holiness of God when he cried *"qadosh, qadosh qadosh yahweh Sabaoth,"* the use of the personal name *YHWH* in Deut. 6.4 has an implicit emphasis on holiness which has been recognized by his people. This holiness affects his uniqueness, oneness, and jealousy. Because he is holy, unique, jealous, and one without comparison he cannot stand what is not perfect and holy.

This holiness is well recognized by the Jewish scribes and worshippers in the synagogue. They believe that the name "Yahweh' is so holy that in order not to profane it, *Adonai* should be mentioned instead. Each time they encounter that would bow down. It is also believed that the avoidance of that name would prevent them from disobeying the First Commandment. The scribes also emphasize the holiness of Yahweh that whenever they copy the Scripture and encounter the name, "Yahweh, they will stop and wash their pens before copying that name. If the name appears ten times their pens would be washed ten times in order not to profane that name.

As stated earlier, the Oneness and uniqueness of Yahweh is paramount in Deuteronomy The word *ehad'means* one and it is used "in contradistinction to many"[19] *He is* not many. Deuteronomy 6:4-9 is essentially saying that there is one Lord, one love and one law. This idea of one Lord also conveys the idea that the same God is unique, different and exclusive.[20] This oneness means that he is not defused or obscured. His person and will are single and known. This YHWH cannot be represented by any image. That is why Deuteronomy and Deuteronomic Historian (DH), demand a centralization of his sanctuary in Jerusalem only. *YHWH*'s singleness includes his uniqueness. Because he is unique, he is the creator and in control of the world. His uniqueness enables him to love

Deuteronomic Conception of God

Israel. Because he is unique, he chose a particular people (Israel) for himself. That is why the concept of election and covenant is very essential to express this, the Hebrew words *bahar* (choose) and (*YHWH berith* -God of the covenant) are used. His uniqueness as the creator gave him, the absolute power to give Israel the land of Canaan, and destroyed the Canaanite since they served another God.

His uniqueness enables Israel to make him a personal God. That is responsible for the use of *Elohim* with the pronominal suffixes and a personal possessive idea of Elohenu *Eloheka* (thy God, our God).[21] There is great repetition of this possessive idea with the use of the word *Elohim* (Deut. 8:5) throughout the book of Deuteronomy.

The singleness and the uniqueness of his purpose, and love for Israel require from his worshippers:

The singleness and uniqueness of purpose.
The singleness and uniqueness of mind.
The singleness and uniqueness of heart
The singleness and uniqueness of soul
The singleness and uniqueness of love.
The singleness and uniqueness of devotion.

In other words, there is a need for absolute loyalty and undivided attention (Deut. 6:5).

The SEMA in African Context.

From the foregoing discussion, it is certain that the importance and the strength of Deuteronomy do not lie in the fact that he is proclaiming an absolute teaching which has not been taught by other Old Testament passages. His strength and importance lie in his persuasive and sermonic presentation of the practical teaching of the Mosaic apodictic and casuistic laws. In so doing, the

Deuteronomic author is able to make use of the experiences of Israel as they encountered *YHWH* and the Canaanite divinities.

From the beginning of Israel's entrance into the land of Canaan, one of the greatest temptations is syncretism. They constantly faced the temptation of worshipping the Canaanite divinities of Baal, and Ashterah. This is the greatest concern of Deuteronomy 6:4 when the author cried "Hear O Israel: The LORD our God is one LORD". As discussed earlier the Deuteronomic author has to remind people constantly that the worshipping of other divinities is not acceptable. According to Deuteronomy, the people addressed are pictured as constantly disobedient, stubborn, and disrespective to God especially by worshipping other gods.

A close examination of this proclamation of Deuteronomy 6:4 shows that the text is very relevant to African Christians today since it is not uncommon to see those who claim to be Christians with a claim of the most holy action, worshipping and making sacrifices to other divinities of African religion. Like the Israelites when they were in Canaan the presence of African divinities has been a constant threat to the majority of those who claim to be Christians from the beginning of the advent of Christianity to the present.[22] With regard to this claim, Harry Sawyer related his experience:

> I have never been able to see any actual performances, but one night, traveling by car up to the college on Mount Auroel, after the midnight hour, my wife and I encountered a woman performing strange antics in the middle of the road just above a second crossroad. One dashed into the tall grass to avoid detention but we identified her before she vanished. She was a regular a professing Christian.[23]

A colleague in the Department of Religions, University of Ilorin, Nigeria also related his most recent experience. He said, that as he was walking to school one day, on reaching a crossroad (*orita*) he saw many cola nuts, oil and salt. When he asked how they got there, he was told that some members of certain churches used them for sacrifices.

Deuteronomy 6:4 have adefinite and straightforward exhortation for those of us in Africa that *YHWH* is one, unique, and jealous. He must be worshipped with undivided attention. To the author of Deuteronomy 6:4, the above practices are not accepted by the unique and one YHWH who is a jealous God.

The author of Deuteronomy never addresses a single person, he addresses the community of elected people of God who have been saved by the grace of God through his covenant. The author of the *SEMA* requires that these people should see themselves as such and act in oneness of mind, soul and heart. Love and unity must permeate his existence. So also the author of the *SEMA* is speaking to us in Africa that as Christians we belong to a community of faith existing by God's grace. There is a need to work in unity, love and singleness of purpose. A certain correspondence between the *SEMA* and the New Testament is evident when Christ proclaims the love of God and fellow men as the greatest commandments. For if we love God we shall definitely love our fellow men.

The use of the personal name *YHWH* also brings a message to our context. According to Deuteronomic theology, the name means practical and active existence and presence with the people of God. In our present situation in Africa especially, as we face economic crisis, the temptation, even with biblical scholars, is to wonder whether God's active presence is with us when some of us found it difficult to feed. The author of the *SEMA* who uses the personal name of God which validates his active presence with us reminds us that YHWH is still actively present with us and his grace and redemptive activity is an ongoing process. For "Tough Times Never Last, But Tough People Do"[24]

As names are significant among the Hebrews, so also are they in Africa. The name *YHWH* does not only mean holiness, it also means power. In Africa, a name is the totality of what a person is.

Endnotes

[1] This article was originally published in Bible Bhashyam (1992), 55-64

[2] David Tuesday Adamo, "The Problem of Translating Hebrew Old Testament into Yoruba Language of Nigeria," *The Bible Translator*, Oct. 1984, vol. 35 no 4.

[3] *The New World Translation* called YHWH, Jehovah.

[4] Alberto Soggin, *Introduction to the Old Testament*. Philadelphia: The Westminster Press, 1976), 115. Otto Eissfeldt, *The Old Testament An Introduction*, Translated by P. R. Ackroyd, (New York: Harper & Row, publishers, 1965) 171. The list of these scholars who accepted de wette's theory are cited by the above authors.

[5] Holscher, "Komposition und Ursprung des Deuteronomiums", *Zeitschrift fur die Affiestamentliche wissenschaft.* 40 (1923), pp. 101-255.

[6] Soggin, *Introduction*, op. cit. 124; Eissfeldt, op. cit, 172 6. Ibid. op. cit.

[7] Eissfeldt, op. cit. 174-175.

[8] Eisdfeldt. op. cit., 174-175.

[9] Ibid. Op. cit.
[10] Ibid., op. cit. 175-176.

[11] B. S. Childs, *Introduction to the Old Testament as Scripture* (Philadelphia: Fortress Press, 1979), 206,207. op. cit,,

[12] Ibid. op. cit. 207-208

[13] M. Weinfeld; "The ' Origin ' of Humanism in Deuteronomy," *Journal of Biblical Literature*, 80 (1961), 241-247

[14] Clifton J. Allen (Gen.) *The Broadman Bible* Commentary (BBC) Vol.. 2 (Nashville: Broadman Press, 1970), 215-216.

[15] George A. Buttrick (Gen. ed.) *Interpreters' Bible* (IB) Vol.2 (Nashville: Abingdon Press, 1953), 373.

[16]Waiter Eichrodt, *Theology of the Old Testament, Vol. 1,* (Philadelphia: The Westministers Press, 1961), 188.

[17]Ibid. 190.

[18]W..F. Albright, *From the stone Age to Christianity* cited in *Theological Wordbook the old Testament.* (eds) R. Harris, O. Archer, B. Walker (Chicago Moody Monthly press, 1980), 285.

[19]*IB.* 373.
[20]*BBC.* 214.
[21]The title *Eloah* may be the singular form of *Elohim* (Deut. 32..15, 17). It later became a synonym of *Elohim*. However, this singular form of, *Elohim* never attain great value like *Elohim*. *Elohim* was first used as an abstract plural or what we might call "plural of intensity" for the purpose of elevating the person designated by the term to a position of representative of his class. In Deut. 6:4, it is used as an abstract plural which corresponds to the word "Godhead" or divinity and to mean that the totality of divine power is brought together in a personal Unity. This term became. very popular to the extent that Elohist used it throughout the Pentateuch to the extent that even after the name Yahweh has been introduced, *Elohim* was retained to designate God side by side with 'Yahweh as it is used in-Deuteronomy 6:4 (*Elohenu*). As it is used, it means the "sum of all Gods, Eichrodt, 188-190.

[22]David. T Adamo,, "The Church. in Africa and African Traditional Religious Beliefs and practices", Unpublished Dissertatiorn, 1985 Rel. D.. Indiana Christian University, Indianapolis. 94.

[23]*Biblical Revelation and African Beliefs* (eds) K. Dickson and
P. Ellingsworth, (New York: Orbis.Books, 1969), 59.

[24]Robert H. Schuler, *Tough Time Never Last, But Tough People Do!* Nashiville : Thomas Nelson Publishers, 1983

PEACE IN THE OLD TESTAMENT AND AFRICAN HERITAGE[1]

Introduction

A close examination of the history of ancient Israel in the period of the Old Testament has shown that ancient Israel constantly faced life of uncertainty. There are actually very few times when she was not in constant wars with the surrounding nations, with far away nations, with Yahweh, and even with herself. Apart from having occasional wars with Philistines, Moabites, Syrians, Amorites, Canaanites, Israel was in perpetual domination of the Assyrians and Babylonians.[2] Israelites were also faced with poverty, oppression, hunger, political instability, and all kinds of evil that one can think of. In the face of all these, peace became an important subject in ancient Israel which kings, priests, prophets and sages not only talked about but also vigorously sought after. Constant wars, hostility, poverty and oppression are not limited to ancient Israel in the period of the Old Testament. Such exist among the modern nations including Israel, Europe, America, Asia, and especially African nations. The present nation of Israel has been faced with constant wars and hostility with their Arab neighbors especially, the Palestinians.³ As a result of this, several peace talks between Israel and her neighbors have also taken place. Although the peace talks have not been successful, it is part of the global attempt to search for peace.

A remembrance of the horror of Nagasai nad Hiroshima during the Second World war in 1945, the present wars and untold suffering in Bosnia, Northern Ireland Iraq and especially in African continents show that peace is not only elusive, it is a rare and urgent commodity that the world needs and must continue to struggle to achieve at all costs.⁴ Certainly, if there is any place where peace is most needed, it is in Africa. Despite the talk about peace, there is still blacks killing blacks, and oppression, in Africa, Angola, Somalia, Sierra Leone and Liberia. In Kenya there is still suffering of tribal clashes, in Zaire and Nigeria, there are political and religious conflicts. Indeed, we cannot mention all the factors of "dis-peace" in the world because they is a disturbingly urgent need for peace all over the world.

In this chapter I attempt to examine the terms used for peace and the general concept of peace in the Old Testament scriptures and in African. Moreover, I suggest what peace' really means and some important factors that may foster 'peace' according to the Old Testament scriptures and from the African perspectives.

The Concept of Peace in the Old Testament

The major term used and translated "peace" in the Old Testament is the Hebrew word *Shalom* and its related words. *Shalom* is one of the very important theological words in the Old Testament. The word occurs more than 250 times in about 213 separate verses.⁵ The King James version (KJV) translates the word Shalom to 'peace' in 172 places.⁶ The related words with the related meaning are Shalem -perfect, whole, full, complete, safe or at peace;

Shelem —peace offering, sacrifice for alliance or friendship or simply to be at peace; *Shallam* —be in covenant of peace or to be at peace with; *Shalmon* -reward, and *Shelomon* — the name of the last king of the United (Israelite) Kingdom which, literally, means 'the man of peace.'[7]

Of the above related words to *Shalom, Shalem* and *Shelem* are the most important. The word *Shalem* seems to express better the concept of *Shalom*.[8] The ideas of wholeness, completeness, harmony, fulfillment that is the root meaning of *shalem* express the meaning of shalom beyond ordinary absence of war. *Shelem* occurs about ninety times in the Old Testament.[9] Scholars' understand *Shelem* mainly in three ways.[10] First, it is said to symbolize a gift of Shalom, which means the blessing of completeness, wholeness, and prosperity and of being at peace with Yahweh. Second, it is believed to mean 'communion sacrifice' where the meat is shared among the people present in the sacrificial place to symbolize fellowship with one another in Yahweh's presence.[11] Third, this has been understood as the concluding sacrifice because Shelem usually comes last in the list of offerings (with exception in Lev. 1-5).[12]

The word *eirene* which means peace in Greek language is used to translate the Hebrew word *Shalom* in the Septuagint (LXX) except where the phrases with Shalom are connected with 'coming and going out and greetings.[13] The etymology of the word *eirene* is uncertain. But it is well known that in the secular language, unlike the word Shalom, the word *eirene* means a state or time of peace. This is always connected with either the cessation of war or the very state or condition, which led to that cessation of war.[14] This may refer to the 'sense of treaty of peace,' the state of rest or a peaceful attitude which led to the interlude in the state of war.[15] However, when the LXX translates the word *Shalom* to *eirene*, it automatically takes on a broader meaning from the profane use. It assumes all the meaning of *Shalom*. This is true where in the LXX, the word Shalom is translated to *eirene* in the passages where the context means wholeness, prosperity and general well being. The LXX uses other Greek words to translate *Shalom*.[16] It uses *te/eios* —' perfect' to translate *shalom* to render one aspect of *Shalom*, 'complete', which is not immediately apparent in *eirene*. The word *Sozo*, salvation, was also used to translate *Shalom* but not as often as *eirene* and *teleios*.

From the above discussion of the various terminologies used for *Shalom*, it is evident that Shalom is a word with a wide comprehensive meaning. It has spiritual, economical, social, physical and eschatological dimension, which shall be discussed below. This means that the word *Shalom*, peace, has a general meaning of all aspect of the state of well-being, that is, completeness, wholeness and everything that brings general well being to the world. Below we shall be concerned with several passages where the word *Shalom* is used with specific meaning from the context. My division of peace into spiritual, social, physical, economical and eschatological dimensions is for convenience sake and for our understanding. These divisions are closely interwoven.

The Spiritual Dimension of Shalom

The spiritual dimension of *Shalom* encompasses all other dimensions. The spiritual dimension of peace includes what Yahweh is Himself, His salvation, His covenant, blessings and everything that Yahweh gives, including prosperity. The spiritual concept of peace in the Old Testament includes Yahweh as peace Himself. In Judges 6:24 Gideon named his altar 'Yahweh is Peace' *(Yahweh Shalom)*. This also means that since Yahweh is Shalom, he is the source and the giver of Shalom and all the goods and values (good health, prosperity, contentment, life and death [Isaiah 5:8; Psalms.38: 3, 4:8].

The spiritual dimension of *Shalom* in the Old Testament is salvific or redemptive. The prophets Jeremiah, Ezekiel and Isaiah are prophets of *Shalom*. These prophets used *Shalom* in the context of salvation. In fact, *Shalom* became the climatic point of their prophetic utterances. The prophet Jeremiah refuted the message of *Shalom* which the false prophets promised Jerusalem 'eternal peace' (emeth Shalom).[16] These false prophets cried 'peace, peace when there is no peace (Jer. 6:14). The prophet Ezekiel also made the same type of complaint saying that the false prophets had led the people astray with their vision of salvation *(Hezon Shalom)* when there was nothing of such. Both Jeremiah and Ezekiel brought the message of *Shalom* in the context of Yahweh's salvation to the climax when they prophesied concerning the exiles of 597 BCE and 586 BCE. Thus Jeremiah can say to the exiles that the thoughts that Yahweh has for them are the thought of *Shalom* (Jer. 29:11). Ezekiel also mentioned the 'covenant of peace' *(berith Shalom), which* Yahweh will make with his people (Ez 34:25; 37:26). According to Isaiah 48:18, if Israel had listened to Yahweh, her *Shalom* would have rolled down like a river. Without any doubt, the use of Shalom by these prophets actually means salvation and should be translated so.[17]

The spiritual dimension of *Shalom* is blessing and righteousness. The concept of *Shalom* as blessing is found in the Holiness Code (Lev. 26:6), with a promise to the people that God will give them shalom in the land of Canaan.[18] Without doubt, the context of the passage shows that the Shalom means solid blessing.[19] The Concept of shalom is also found at the climax of blessing in Numbers 6:24ff. Here all other blessings are summed up: " The LORD bless you and keep you: The LORD make his face to shine upon you, and be gracious to you: The Lord lift up his countenance upon you, and give you peace."

Shalom is also connected with righteousness. The *shalom* promised Jerusalem is associated with righteousness (I Sam. 54:13 and 32: 17). The Hebrew sometimes uses *Shalom* when there is a reference to covenant (berth). Two possibilities of the exact meaning of this connection are apparent.[20] First, possibly the relation of *Shalom* is sealed by both parties in a covenant. Second, maybe the covenant is an inauguration of a relationship of *shalom.* Whichever way the connection is understood the relationship is a strong one and *Shalom has* become *an official term in this relationship.* The prophet Ezekiel is especially emphatic about this covenant of peace. According to him the covenant of peace is not a material but a spiritual well being. [21] It is a covenant of peace between Yahweh and His people, Israel Deutero-Isaiah also mentions this *berith Shalom* when he says: 'My kindness shall not depart from thee, neither shall the covenant of my peace be removed' (RSV. Isa. 54:10).

The spiritual concept of shalom has an eschatological aspect. We find in the Old Testament that there is a strong expectation of a final state of eternal *shalom.* This is evident in the declaration by the prophets Isaiah of Jerusalem and Zechariah. There is an expectations of the Messiah who is supposed to be David's grandson whose name will be 'Prince of Peace' (Sar Shalom)[22] He will be the one who is to bring fulfillment and righteousness to the world. This proclamation of the Messiah who will bring the eternal shalom is not limited to the prophet Isaiah; the prophet Zechariah also has an expectation of the time of international peace.[23] The prophets Hosea, Isaiah, and Amos also prophesized the condition in paradise or of international peace under a divine direction.[24]

The Qumran, community without any doubt believed that they were the eschatological community of those who are already saved. They saw themselves as having already entered into the very eschatological peace promised in the Old Testament (IQS 8:4-9; CD. 1:4). In several of their writings there are references to eternal peace 'peace without end', lasting peace, and 'super-abundance of peace'.[25]

The Social Dimension of Shalom

The observation by some commentators that *Shalom* in its most common use is emphatically a social concept is evident in the understanding of *Shalom* as an absence of war, a relationship between fellow people and nations, and its link with righteousness, covenant, and judgement. A close examination of the use of *shalom* shows that it means absence of strife in approximately fifty to sixty times in the Old Testament.'[26] The translation of *Shalom* to *eirene* in the LXX supports the strong meaning of Shalom as cessation of war. In fact, in 'profane' Greek and from Homer onward the word *eirene* primarily and strictly means the 'antithesis of war or the condition resulting from cessation of war.'[27] In the Old Testament, *shalom* does not only mean an absence of war, but all kind of strife or strained relationships. It means good relations between nations and between men and women (I Kgs 5:26, Jdg 4:17 and I Chron. 12:17-18). It denotes security, opposite of disorder of any kind and harmony among men or 'unimpaired relationship with others'.[28]

Although, the covenant aspect of *Shalom* is spiritual as discussed above, it also has a social aspect. That peace marks the conclusion of a covenant between enemies (Gen. 26:29) and business partners (1 Kgs. 5:12) is the social aspect *of Shalom*. Such covenant of people guarantees good relationship between nations, men, women, and brothers. In its social aspect, *Shalom* is the result of righteousness (Isa. 32.17) and judgement (Zech 8:16). The Hebrew word for righteousness is *Sedaqa* or *Sedeq* and for judgment is *mispath*. The usages of these words occur in relation to the function of judges.[29] It has the idea of discharging the truth and making decisions without partiality. The righteousness in relation to *Shalom* describes three aspect of relationships — 'ethical. forensic and theocratic.[30] The ethical aspect, which involves human relationship, is our main concern because it describes the social aspect of *Shalom*. It is the 'quality of relationships between individuals by adhering to certain norm in the society.' The person who is righteous preserves and maintains the Shalom and prosperity of a community. In the highest sense, the man or woman who serves God by delivering the poor, the orphans, and the blinds supports the weak performs the the social dimension of *shalom*.[31] The *Saddiq* gives freely without regard to gain (Ps. 37:21). Such person promotes peace, blessing and exaltation of a nation. Such is the message of the Old Testament prophets who cry for righteousness, justice throughout the land. The forensic aspect deals with equality of all, rich or poor before the law.[32] The righteous man shall not die for he keeps the law (Ex. 23:7). The theocratic aspect of righteousness is the covenant between Yahweh and the nation of Israel, which requires obedience to God (Ps 1:1-6; Deut. 6:25).[33]

As discussed earlier, the social aspect of *Shalom* is the most common usage. This social concept is not only the covenantal peace, absence of war, righteousness, but also to wish someone well. As in modern Hebrew where *Shalom* is used for greeting such as 'hello', goodbye', for about twenty-five times in Old Testament, the word *Shalom* means greetings or farewell (Jdg. 19:20, 1 Sam. 25. 6-25).[34] In the Old Testament, to wish one *Shalom*, is to bestow on such a person blessing and peace (II Sam 15:27). To withhold *Shalom* implies a curse (I Kgs. 2:6). In the Rabbinical Literature the word *Sa'al besalom* 'to greet,' means to ask after someone's peace or to wish it for someone.[35]

The Economic Dimension of Shalom

There is also the economic concept of *Shalom* in the Old Testament. The general meaning of *Shalom* and its various aspect means wholeness, safety as well as prosperity and good physical health. The blessing, which Yahweh promised his people, is unlimited. It includes economic prosperity. The *Shalom* that Yahweh gave included the land of Canaan, good health and other material prosperity (Ps. 73:3). The *Shalom* which Solomon and Hiram (I Kgs. 5:12) enjoyed is considered in the Old Testament as the blessing of Yahweh. [36] It describes Solomon's peace by recounting his wealth:

> His insight into the strategic virtue of his territory and his monopolistic control of the ancient near eastern trade routes plus his important copper mining from south of the Dead Sea and all his metal working, enabled him to

sustain a large standing army and to construct and maintain the fortified cities (eg. Megiddo, Hazor, Eglon. Gezer), that guaranteed his independence.[37]

The Concept of Peace in Africa

Although Kwensi Dickson admitted the fact that there are similarities between the Old Testament and African life and thought, he cautioned scholars who might want to undertake the task of comparing them.[38] This caution is as a result of the fact that the events in the Old Testament, although have a universal application, happened in a particular location to a particular people and under a different culture from Africa. [39]Although there are differences, the similarities are overwhelming. This is especially true of the concept of 'peace.' Like the Old Testament, African religious heritage has spiritual, economic and social dimension of *Shalom*.

An African scholar has defined 'peace' as 'that thing which we all need and desire, which we do not have, which is painfully and destructively lacking in the world.'[40] A critical survey of the world situation, especially of factors that contribute to 'dis-peace', will certainly convince us that this definition is in one way appropriate. Chaos, confusion, war, violence, corruption, oppression are all over the world. In further attempt to define 'peace' positively, Dr, Dime continues: 'Peace means public order, calmness of mind, amity, harmony in person, concord, tranquility, wholeness, well being and security.[41] Africans attach great importance to *Shalom*. To all Africans, *shalom* is the sum-total of what any person may desire including all that constitutes life, good health, shelter, food, and prosperity. To Africans, *Shalom* also means completeness, wholeness and the totality of good life. This definition of *Shalom* is graphically illustrated by a Yoruba common song and saying:

Maa Kole, mao bimo, maa ra moto ayokele,
Laisi alafia, Won yen ko sese
Alafia loju. Ilera loro.

Eniti O ni alafia O lohun ,gbogbo. [42]

Translation:

> I will build a house
> I wilt bear children
> I will buy motorcars
> Without peace *(Shalom)*
> Those things are impossible
> Peace *(Shalom)* is the most important
> Health is wealth
> He who has peace *(Shalom)*
> Has everything' [43]

When one meditates on the above definitions and the importance of *Shalom*, one is bound to ask these questions: Is there real *Shalom* on earth? Can there be *Shalom* on earth?

The Spiritual Dimension of Peace in Africa

The spiritual dimension of *Shalom* in Africa is greatly determined by African Traditional Religion and Culture. By African Traditional Religion (ATR) I mean, in line with Idowu and Awolalu:

> The indigenous religion of the Africans is the religion that has been handed down from generation to generation by the forbears of the present generation of Africans. It is not a fossil religion (a thing of the past), but a religion that Africans today have made theirs of living it and practicing it. This is a religion that has no written literature yet it is written" everywhere for those who care to see and read. It is largely written in the peoples myth and folklores.'[44]

Indigenous Africans believe in the existence of the Supreme Being, the divinities, the spirits and the ancestors. It is strongly believed that the Supreme Being who is the creator of the heaven and the earth, and the person who orders all things as He wishes, is the giver of *Shalom.*. Rain, increase in family, cattle, good crops, and happiness are given by the Supreme Being. In the organization and administration of the world, are the divinities that He has created to act as ministers or functionaries in His universe.

For the blessing of *shalom*, homage is paid to the Supreme Being through these divinities. Whoever wants *Shalom* must keep in touch with the divinities that are believed to carry man's requests to the Supreme Being. Since some of these divinities are believed to be avengers of evil and crime, they are to be appeased through mediators who are able to find peace out of their expectation. Regular worship is expected to abound in the community. Apart from the Supreme Being, the divinities and the spirits, are the ancestors who can be of tremendous help to those who obey the family taboos and keep them. They can also exert punishment on those who disobey. Indigenous African society therefore, seeks the guidance of the Supreme Being and His functionaries for the maintenance of *Shalom*. To them, the owners of true *Shalom*, are the Supreme Being and His functionaries. Humankind only needs to play its part.

In African Traditional Society, justice is immediate and if delayed can have grave consequences. To them, justice delayed is justice denied.' The Supreme Being and His functionaries strictly adhere to honesty, faithfulness, integrity, sincerity and loyalty to one another, which are the essential ingredient for Shalom in African Traditional society for the fear of punishment. Such fear controls the individual's entire life. Dr. Dime narrates the experience of a Chief Justice in a customary court. The chief testified that during his forty years experience in court, evidence of witnesses sworn on African Traditional Religious symbols like cutlasses or guns were found to be 'the truth and the whole truth,' whereas those sworn on the Holy Bible or Koran told 'tissues of lies' and studied falsehood with gross impunity.[45]

Likewise, Professor Segun Ogungbemi narrated his experience in his village: Several years ago, some new electric generators belonging to a local Church in Nigeria were stolen, and all efforts to recover them were unsuccessful. Not long afterwards, a costume belonging to Origha's divinity at Idofin village was stolen. When the priest of *Origba* and the people became aware of it, they alerted the entire village and warned the thief of the consequence. When nobody heeded the warning, all of a sudden, there was lightning and thunder. Quickly, the costume of divinity of *Origba* was returned. [46]

In the olden days items for sale could be left on the roadside with a number of small stones indicating the price of the items. Whoever buys pays the exact price and keeps the money in place of the goods. But today, it is the opposite. What I have been trying to say is that in African traditional society where African Traditional Religion and culture is strictly adhered to, honesty, sincerity, loyalty and faithfulness prevail.

This ensures Shalom in African traditional society; covenant making is synonymous to *berith Shalom* in the Old Testament, which I have already discussed. Every clan or society has a divinity to which they are bound through covenant. For example the worshippers of Ogun divinity (god of Iron or of war) among the Yoruba of Nigeria, bound themselves with covenant to be one, to seek the welfare of one another, forbidden to harm one another, forbidden to Commit adultery with the wife of Ogun worshipper or hunter. [47] It is believed that whoever breaks the covenant would be punished by death. Dime rightly observed that:

Today, on the other hand, our society with countless policemen and soldiers is plagued with armed robbery, avarice, bribery and corruption, embezzlement of public funds, widespread sexual immorality, even homosexuality and lesbianism at all tenets of society, cases of murder for various materials ends, indiscipline in institution of higher learning, high and low, shameless desecration of holy places and conscienceless breach of contracts. When the traditional society was strictly faithful to its religion those crimes were very rare indeed.[48]

The Social Dimension of Peace in Africa

In African context there is a social dimension of peace. *Shalom* is not simply the absence of war, it also means tolerance and respect for one another. This tolerance is an important aspect of shalom. This is rooted in the teaching of African Traditional Religion. Religious intolerance, that is, my religion is the only right one, or the best, has led the world into chaos. It has led to the barbaric institution in which many devoted ones have been murdered.[49] It has led to the crusades during the medieval period.[50] The war in Northern Ireland and the yearly destruction of lives by religious fanatics in Northern Nigeria are caused by terrible religious intolerance.

The African Traditional Religious spirit of tolerance and openness was demonstrated by their unparalleled hospitality in the 19th century during the advent of Christian missionaries. For example, Ifa oracle was consulted during the coming of the Christian missionaries. The response was a prediction of their coming and that they should be received with open arms. In 1842, at Ikare. They came and were warmly received and well protected.[51] This tolerance was also extended to both Islam and Christianity in the Southern part of Nigeria (Ikare, Ondo state). At Ikare during Ileya, a Moslem annual festival, many Christians participated in the celebrations. During fasting, both African traditionalists and Christians ate together with the Moslems. To my amazement Christmas and the New Year were celebrated together with the Moslems.

Another social aspect of *Shalom* in Africa is greeting. In African Traditional culture, greeting is taken very seriously. Like the Hebrew Conception of *Shalom*, greeting means more than just hello. Among the Yoruba people of Nigeria one greets: *Se alafia ni?* Among the Hausa in Nigeria, one greets: *ina Kwana?* Which literally means 'are you in good health?' Then one answers: *Lafia lau*, that is, 'I am **in** peace' or 'I am in good health.' The Ibo of Nigeria will greet: *Kedu Kodu* —which literally means 'How are you' or

'How is your peace?' In all the major three languages of Nigeria, greetings mean enquiring about one's peace. In fact, it goes beyond such enquiry: When you greet someone, the greeting suggests that there is peace between you and the person you greet. If one person meets another, and does not greet, it means there is no peace between them. The importance of greetings among the Yoruba and the Hausa can be seen in the length of time spent in greetings. If you visit Nigeria, do not be surprised if you happen to meet two or more people, right in the middle of the road, kneeling down, asking about children, wife, husbands, sisters, brothers, even cows and others. Such greetings may even take as long as fifteen to thirty minutes.

In Kiswahili, the word *Salama* is very close to the Arabic *Salaam* and the Hebrew *Shalom* —which literally mean 'peace' or 'good health.' Among the Luo of Kenya, the expression *'idhi nade?'* means 'how have you been?' Among the Luhya of Kenya, I understand that the expression *muli abalamu?* for greetings literally means 'how are you?' While the Gikuyu of Kenya would greet: *Muriega? —* 'are you in peace?' the Kalenjin would greet: *Chain gei? —* 'how are you?' In the expressions of greeting cited above, there are some elements of enquiring about somebody's well being or pronouncing peace on somebody.

The Economic Dimension of Peace in Africa

In the western world, the question of daily food, normal clothing, school fees, from primary school to high school are taken for granted. For example, in USA there are 'food stamps' for those who are unemployed. Tuition in Primary schools and high schools in state institutions is affordable. Most of the basic needs in daily life are provided by the state. The affluent nations of the North Atlantic region have established welfare systems to meet the basic necessities for their citizens. Thus the people in the affluent nations are able to devote their efforts in pursuit of secondary desires and inventions. In Africa, however, our major daily struggle is the search for basic necessities — food, water, shelter, clothes, fuel, health, and education. As a result of this daily struggle, peace in the contemporary African society has an important economic dimension and it means, very importantly, the basic means of survival. Without these, there is nothing like 'peace' to any African

The economic dimension of *Shalom* is the most important meaning of peace, followed by the spiritual dimension. There will always be chaos whenever these dimensions are lacking, ignored or overlooked. *Shalom* in African context means proper leadership and proper management. I strongly believe that the major problem in Africa is not lack of economic resources but l lack of proper management of such resources and 'good' leadership. Proper management would enhance peace and justice. Peace in this case will mean the possibiglity of human development that touches all human needs. Greed, selfishness, corruption, injustice conflict division, poverty and untold human suffering would be minimized if there exist 'good leadership.

Conclusion

What I have been saying about *Shalom* according to both the Old Testament and African concepts is that *Shalom* has spiritual, social, and economic aspects. *Shalom* are not simply an absence of war, but absence of fear, tension and mutual mistrust. *Shalom* is everything that makes life liveable. In fact, it can be described as life itself, which, according to both the Old Testament and African traditional society, is the gift of God. If *shalom* means the complete well being of humanity, do we have *Shalom?* Can we ever have *Shalom* in this confused world? There is a temptation to answer negatively. However, if Yahweh is *Shalom* Himself, is it impossible for Him to bring shalom to the world? If Yahweh would bring *shalom*, He will use His people on earth. It will mean that the religious leaders who preach *shalom* in Churches, mosques, temples and shrines but do exactly the opposite [52] of what they preach should stop such hypocritical action, if Yahweh is to use them for ushering in the *shalom*. Christian leaders must be awakened to their prophetic calling to defend the truth and justice inside and outside their Churches in order for the true *shalom* to be realized in our world.

Endnotes

[1] This article was formerly published in *The Bible in African Christianity: Essays in Biblical Theology*, edited by H.W Kinoti and J.M Waliggo, Nairobi, Kenya: Acton Publishers, 1997, 99-112

[2] Referring especially to the captivity, the Deuteronomic historians were emphatic that Israel went through these wars as a result of their sin. Ancient Israel also spent most of her life as vassals where the Assyrians eventually destroyed the Northern Kingdom in 721 BCE, and the Babylonians finally destroyed the Southern kingdom in 586 BCE.

[3] Israel's expulsion of 417 Palestinians to 'No-man's Land' in Lebanon (which was widely criticized in the international forum), is an example of the state of hostility in the region.

[4] Credit must be given to the United Nations for alt their efforts to restore peace all over the world.

[5] R.L. Harris, G.L. Archer, Jr and B.K. Waltke, 'Shalom', *Theological Wordbook of the Old Testament* (Chicago: Moody Bible Institute, 1981), 2401. —henceforth TWOT; Colin Brown, General Editor, 'Peace', *The New International Dictionary of the New Testament*, —henceforth NIDNTT (Grand Rapids; Zondervan Publishing House, 1982),776-777. F. Brown, SR. Driver and CA. Briggs, *Hebrew and English Lexicon of the Old Testament* — henceforth BDB (Oxford: Claredon Press, 1977), 1022 says that *shalom* occurs 237 times.

[6] *TWOT.*, 2401

[7] *TWOT.*, 2401
[8] *TWOT.*, 2399-2402 and BDB., 1022-1024.

[9] Ibid.
[10] Ibid.
[11] de Vauz supports this, see ibid, 2402

Peace in the OT and Africa

¹²Ibid.

¹³Example of this place is Gen. 26: 31, 43:23; Jer. 20:10, Isa. 48:22; 57:2t, See 'Peace' NIDNTT vol. 2, 777

¹⁴Werner Foerster, editor G. Kittel, *Theological Dictionary of the New Testament,* Vol. II Translated by Geoffrey W. Bromiley, (Grand Rapids: WM B. Eerdmans Publishing Company, 1982),400-411, henceforth IDNT. See also H. H. Beck and C., Brown, 'Peace,' *IDNT,* 401.

¹⁵Kings 8:16, II: 4, 15:3; 1 Chro. 28:9; Deut. 28:13; Jer. 13:19; Ex. 12:5.

¹⁶Jer. 14:13.

¹⁷In several places some of these prophetic use of Shalom should be translated salvation instead of peace (e.g. Jer. 29:11). Jeremiah was speaking to those who were in exile in Babylon.

¹⁸von Rad, *Eirene IDNT.* 404.

¹⁹In the Rabinnical literature the words *Shalom* and *berakah* — 'blessing' correspond because they are the gifts of Yahweh to his people — von Rad, *TDNT,* 409.

²⁰von Rad, *TDNT,*403

²¹Ez.34:25; 37:26.

²²Isaiah 9:5-6. See also G.L CaiT, 'Shalom', *TWOT,* 2401. While Judaism still expects the Messiah, Christians believe in Jesus Christ as the fulfillment of the messianic expectation.

²³Zech 9:10. Although the word *shalom* does not occur in Zech. 9:10 and Isa 2:2ff, that does not make the proclamation of *shalom* in those texts less important.

²⁴²⁴Isa. t:lff, Hosea 2:2Off, Amos 9:l3ff.

²⁵IQS 2:4; IQH 15:16; IQH 18:30; IQS 4:7. See also H.Bech and C.Brown, 'Peace', NIDNiT,) Vol. 2, 779

²⁶Example of these usages are in I Kings 4:25. See also G.L. Carr, TWOT, 2401.

²⁷H. Beck and C.Brown, 'Peace,' N1DN17T, Vol 2., 776.

²⁸The New Testament catches these meanings more appropriately Lk.14:32, Lk.

12:20; Lk. 11:21 and Acts 24:2,1 Cor. 14:33, Acts 7:26, Gal 5:22; Eph. 4:3 James. 3:18.

[29]H.G. Stigers, Sadeq' *TWOT*, Vol 2, 1870. The masculine 'Sedeq' occurs 118 times. The feminine *'Sedaqa'*, 156 times. In its original meaning, it basically connotes conformity to a moral standard or to be straight or norm.

[30]*Ibid*.

[31]Ibid.
[32]Ibid.
[33]Ibid., 1876.
[34]G.L Carr, "*Shalom*", *TWOT*, Vol 2, 2401
[35]H. Beck, and C. Brown, 'Peace,' NIDNTT, Vol. 2, 777
[36]Ibid. Solomon and Hiram were trade partners.
[37]"Shalom," *TWOT*, Vol. 2, 2402.
[38] 'Continuity and Discontinuity between the Old Testament and African Lifeand Thought', in Kofi Appiah Kubi and Sergio Torres. eds, *African, Theologyen Route*, (New York: Orbis Books.1979),97-98

[39]Ibid.
[40] C.A. Dime, "African Religion in the Quest For Peace", in Sam Babs Mala and Z.I Oseni, eds. *Religion Peace and Unity in Nigeria* (Ibadan: Nigerian Association for the Study of Religions (NASR), 1984.7

[41]Ibid., 8
[42]Ibid., The Yoruba people are in South West of Nigeria.
[43]Dr. Dime's translation is not accurate. The translation is mine. See ibid.
[44]J.O Awolalu, "Sin and its Removal in African Traditional Religion", *Journal of the American Academy of Religion*, Vol. 44, no 2, (1976), 275.
[45]Dime.
[46]At the time of writing Prof. Segun Ogungbemi was Associate Professor and Head of Department of Philosophy, Moi University, Eldoret. Idofin is in Kogi State of Nigeria.
[47]Dime., 15.
[48]Ibid
[49]F.L Cross, ed. "Inquisition," *Oxford Dictionary of the Christian Church* (Oxford: Oxford University Press, 1977), 705-706.
[50]Ibid. "Crusades," 362-363. See also Latourette, *A History of Christianity*, Vol. II (New York: Harper and Row, 1975), 408-415.
[51]F.D Walker, *Hundred Years in Nigeria*, (Cargate Press, 1942), 24-26. See also Dime, 18-19. Ifa Oracle is an oracular divinity of the Yoruba people of Nigeria.

SPIRIT (*RUACH*) IN THE OLD TESTAMENT AND IN AFRICAN CONTEXT[1]

Introduction

The term ruach means wind, breath, air or spirit, It is one of the terms which belong to an important aspect of the Hebrew psychology. Other important terms are *nephesh*, which means soul, *baser*, flesh or body, and *leb*, which basically mean heart. The above terms used in the Hebrew psychology reflect the nature of man.

These terms belong to that branch of anthropology that interprets the ideas held about human personality.[2] The ancient Hebrew concept of man is very much like that of the primitive people of the ancient and modern peoples of the world.[3] Although the Hebrew psychology does not refer to a completely organized and scientific explanation of consciousness, the basic assumption that man is a unitary being is prominent. Edmond Jacob describes this:

> Man is a psycho-physical being and phsychical functions are bound so closely to its physical nature that they are all localized in bodily organs which themselves, only draw their life from vital force that animates them.[4]

The Old Testament does not see man as autonomous, or in a piecemeal fashion but in totality. Man's consciousness in diffused throughout his whole body so that the different parts of the body have a quasi-consciousness of their own.[5] The prophets of the Old Testament think of man as an animated body with many parts that can function in quasi-independence of one another.[6] Man is a unity with the body with a complex parts. These parts draw their life from the breath soul that has no existence apart from the body.[7] Certainly, there is, at times, a confusion and fluidity in the use of the terms mentioned above in the Hebrew psychology, despite the understanding of man as a unitary being. This makes it impossible to discuss *ruach* in isolation. Therefore, the discussion of *ruach* will automatically include a discussion of the basic important terms in the Hebrew psychology (*nephesh, basar* and *Leb*). However, more emphasis will be laid on *ruach* as it relates to these terms.

Nephesh, Basar and Leb

Nephesh

The word *nephesh* occurs 755 times in the Old Testament.[8] It is one of the basic words of the Old Testament anthropology which is generally translated "Soul" in the English Bible. In the LXX Out of 755 occurences, it is translated *Psyhe (Soul)*.[9] However, the word *nephesh* does not always mean "Soul." According to Von Rad, the word in most places is wrongly translated Soul.[10] According to von Rad, the word originally meant throat, but because the throat is the organ of breathing it later attained the idea of "breath" which comes out of the throat.[11] The breath, which comes out of the throat, was later identified with life since when one dies, there is no more breath from the throat. Thus the *nephesh* can be identified with the principle of life.[12] The above means that the word *nephesh* means several different things in the Bible. In each case, the textual context decides how it is to be translated. The different meanings of *nephesh* are as follows: - The word *Nephesh* in Isaiah 5:14 means throat when it says:

Spirit in the OT and in Africa

> "Therefore hell has enlarged its throat, and opened its mouth beyond measure; and the nobility of Jerusalem and her multitude go down her throng and he who rejoiceth exults in her" (RSV).

According to the above passage, the mouth is wide opened to swallow. This is a clear indication that the word *nephesh* refers to a gullet or throat. In the same way Habakkuk 2:5 talks about a rapacious man opening his *nephesh* wide as hell and death, but never get satisfied. Other passages include Psalm 107:5,9; Ecclesiastes, 6:7,9 which talk about the *nephesh* as the insatiable desire of the throat.

Nephesh can also mean the outer neck in several occasions. In this case neck is referred to by the *nephesh* and not Soul as popularly believed. Psalm 105-18 says "His feet were hurt with fetters, his neck *(nephesh)* came into form. That the word *nephesh* here means neck is clear by both the word "iron" and feet. Other passages where the word *nephesh* can mean neck are I Sam. 28:9, Psalm 124:7 and Psalm 44:25.

The word *nephesh* can also mean a desire. This means that *nephesh*, can refer to the organ of taste. In several places, the *nephesh* yearns with his desire *(nephesh)* for food and preservation of life. This yearning, desiring or striving is referred to a *nephesh*. This is the case in Psalm 35:25, Prov. 23:2. "You have put a knife to your throat if you are a Baal *nephesh*, (Prov. 23:2). In this context it is the lust that is thought of as *nephesh*.[13]

Nephesh can also mean feelings or soul. One of the places where we can translate *nephesh as* soul or feeling is in Exodus 23:9. It says:

> You shall not oppress a stranger,
> You know the soul *(nephesh)* of a stranger,
> For you were strangers in the land of Egypt.

Here the Writer is certainly not thinking about the stranger's need or desires, but of these feelings, of his soul. According to Job, the central organ of a suffering man is his soul. He asked, "How will you torment my nephesh?" The typical organ of sympathy with the needy is the Soul (Job 30:25). Other passages include Job 2:7, Prov. 3:16; 11 Samuel 5:8.

In several places, the word *nephesh*, can mean throat, neck, desire, or soul, but also life itself in its entirety. Proverbs 8:3 says: "He who finds me has found life and has obtained favor from Yahweh, but he who misses me violates his *nephesh* (life)." In Leviticus 24:17, it is clear that *nephesh* here means life in its entirety. He who kills the *nephesh* of man shall be put to death. He who kills the *nephesh* of a beast shall make it good. Here it means life is for life in the case of vengeance.

Basar

The word *basar* occurs 273 times in the Old Testament. Out of this 273 times, 104 of these aplies to animals. It is also noteworthy that whereas *nephesh*, applies to God in about 3% of the occurrences in the Old Testament, the word *basar* never applies to God. What this means is that the word *basar* is strictly a terminology of both man and beast.[14] *Basar* therefore, denotes all living creatures. In this case, the translation of the word is "flesh". Interestingly the Hebrew word does not have any word of body in the sense that the Greek *Soma is* used. In the Old Testament body and soul are so united in such a way that it is difficult to make any distinction between the two.[15] *Basar is* used to mean flesh in Isaiah 22:13 when he describes Jerusalem's carelessness: Behold joy and carelessness, slaying oxen and killing sheep eating *basar* drinking wine. "Let us eat and drink for tomorrow we die."

It is clear here that *basar* means a flesh of a slaughtered beast. Isaiah 44:16 talks about the meat that is eaten roasted. Job 41:23 also talks of the *basar* of a crocodile. The mentioning of *basar* includes the *basar* of sacrificial animals in ritual regulation (Lev. 4:1 7:15-21). *Basar* also means the flesh of man or the body or skin. *Basar* is also used to refer to a small portion of the skin or

Spirit in the OT and in Africa

body. In a way the *basar* of the foreskin is mentioned in Gen. 17:11, 14. In Lev. 15 , cf., 7, 19 male and female organs are referred to as *basar*.

Basar is also used for human body as a whole. In Number 8:7 during the Levite consecration, one should not allow razor go over their *basar*, that is, the whole body. In Lev. 13:2ff a distinction is made between the skin of the body and the hair on it (V. 4). However, in Lev. 19-28 *basar* means both the body and the hair on it.

Basar can also mean fellowship rather than flesh. Gen. 2:24 says that a man and a woman cleaving together shall become one *basar*. This basar means a common body, a fellowship for life. Basar is therefore used in the sense of what binds people together. In Gen. 37:27 Judah pointed out that Joseph, their brother was their own *basar*, that is, the nearest relation. *Basar* can also mean 'Weakness. That is why Wolff sees *basar* as a man in his own infirmity.[16] Psalm 56:4 confesses: "In God I hope without a fear. What can *basar* do to me?" Jer. 17:5,7 says: "Cursed is the man who trusts in man and makes basar his arm.... Blessed is the man who trusts in Yahweh." I Chron. 32:8 says: "With him is but an arm of flesh; but with us in Yahweh our God, to help us." Thus in the Old Testament we see *basar* to mean also "the powerlessness of the mortal creature," and the feebleness of his faithfulness.[17]

Leb.

Wolff sees the term *Leb* as the most important term of the Old Testament anthropology. *Leb* with its other variant (*lebab*) occurs 858 times n the Old Testament.[18] This then makes it to be the most common of all the anthropological terms in the Old Testament.

The word *leb* or *lebab* in contrast to other main anthropological terms almost exclusively refers to man. It applies to animals only 5 times and four of these instances are in comparison to human's heart. The most common translation is heart. The word *leb* is so crucial that its importance cannot be overemphasized. This importance can be seen in the strong emotion that is physically felt in the *leb*. There is hardly any spiritual process, which could be brought into some connection with the heart.[19] It is made both the organ of feelings, intellectual activities, and the working of the will.[20]

In this regard the word *leb* is used to mean the heart, gut feelings, wish, reason, and will, in the Old Testament. The most interesting passage where the Old Testament described its understanding of the heart is in I Sam. 25: 37-38. ".... his (*leb*) died within him, and he became as a stone. And about ten days later the Lord smote Nabal; and he died. (RSV.).

In the above passage the Hebrew writer does not talk about *leb* to mean heartbeat, or brain, or nerves, or lungs, but his central organ, which made limbs possible to move.[21] This part, which refers to heart in the passage above, corresponds with certain part of the brain (cerebrum). This is true when one remembers that Nabal's heart died but he still lived up to ten days. The passages which reflect this Hebrew understanding of heart are Jeremiah 14:19, 23:9, Proverbs 30:18, and Psalm 38:10. This is understood this way because the people of ancient Israel did not understand the anatomy of the body as in the modern scientific way.

The word *leb* also means feelings. When mentioned in this case, they talk about *leb*, which affects the sensibility and the emotions of the people. This concerns what the modern man will ascribe to feeling and mood, "the irrational level of man."[22] Psalm 25:17 talks about the sick heart: "Relieve the troubles of my heart, and bring me out of my distresses." Here the first sentence *sarot lebabi harheb* actually means, "expand the narrow places of my heart." This refers to a cry of pain. Proverb 15:3 and 23: 17 mention *leb* to mean feeling or emotion. "A glad heart (*leb*) makes a cheerful countenance, but by a sorrow of heart the Spirit is broken" (15:13 RSV). Proverbs 17:22 also says: "....A cheerful heart promotes health....

The word *leb* also means wish. Just as in the wish of

Spirit in the OT and in Africa

nephesh, one can talk about wish, desire or longing with *leb*." Pslam 21:2 say: " Thou hast given him his hearts desire (leb) and has not withheld the request of his lip. This perhaps refers to inner secret wishes since it talks to a heart very close to lips." *Leb* can also mean reason. By far this is the greatest number of cases it is used as intellectual and rational function ascribed to heart. This is what the modern man will ascribe to head and brain. This connotation is reflected over and over in several passages. Proverb 15:14 described what is essentially the function of the heart as the seeking of knowledge. Compare Proverb 8:5; 18:15; 16:23 which describe the heart of the wise who makes his speech judicious.

Ruach

My discussion so far has been on the words *nephesh*, *basar* and *leb*. This is deliberate, because these words will form a background to a better understanding of our assigned word, *ruach*. The words discussed earlier will surely enhance our understanding of *ruach* because in several of these usages they are synonymous, though wrongly translated in several versions. That is, they can be used interchangeably. What appears to be responsible for this is the fact that they all belong to the same Hebrew psychological terms. Thus, they are affected by the Hebrew concept of cooperate personality. Most of these similarities in meanings will be clearly discussed in this section on *ruach*.

The noun *ruach* is usually feminine in the Old Testament. While some people derived this noun from *rawah* which means "to be spacious, be refreshed" (I Sam. 16:23; Job 23:20), it should be more appropriately considered a primitive noun closely related to an *ayin* verb, *ruh* to breathe." This root is very likely when one compares the word *reah*, "odor" and the ugaritic word *rh*.[23]

Despite these similarities in usages, there are some

factors, which distinguish *ruach* from *nephesh, basar* and *leb*. Wolff discusses these distinguishable factors as follows.[24] The statistical examination of the use of *ruach* makes these distinguishable factors clear. *Ruach*, to a large extent, is a term used for "natural power" meaning "wind" (will be elaborated below). This term does not apply less than 113 out of 389 times used in the Old Testament. Another interesting distinguishable factor is the fact that *ruach* refers to God more often than to men, animals or gods. It refers to God 136 times and 129 times to animals and gods.

What I am saying above is that while *nephesh* applies to God in about 3% of its occurrences, and *basar* never applies to God at all, *ruach* applies to God 35 % of its usages, in the Old Testament. This is the reason Wolff calls *ruach* "a theo-anthropological term."[25] I shall discuss more elaborately the various usages of *ruach*.

In African religious tradition, the word *ruach* or spirit is called *emi* in Yoruba religion in Nigeria. Spirits are common and worshipped. *Ruach* in African belief are apparitional entities, which are of different category of being. Though these spirits are anthropomorphically conceived as if they are abstract beings, it is believed that they are capable of becoming whatever they want to become. Sometimes they become objects, wind, vapor, ghost, trees, human being, water and as many things as one can name. It is also believed that all things and places have spirits of their own. Trees, rocks, mountains, hills, forests, and rivers have spirits. These spirits are nameless beings, even though they are often identified with certain objects, which they inhabit. As nameless as they may be they have categories by which they can be described.

The first category of spirit in African tradition can be called ghost -spirits. These are the spirit of the departed who wander about. It is believed that a person who dies and was not given a special burial may wander around. This includes someone who is totally wicked and died a bad death.

The second category of spirits is the born-to-die

Spirit in the OT and in Africa

spirits. The Yoruba and Ibo people call this *abiku* and *ogbanje* respectively. These are sadistic spirits who wander around and eventually enter a pregnant woman to be born as children and to torture the family. No matter how you take care of them medically, they would die. Pregnant women are warned not to walk around at night and at certain time of the day, usually at noon.

The third category of spirits is spirits that are also painfully real to Africans. They are terribly disastrous and are greatly feared because of the harm they inflict on people. They are capable of being in places at any time in a twinkling of an eye. Their food is to suck the blood of their victim. These are spirit of witches and they are real in Africa.

The fourth category is the guardian spirits. They are important spirits that are inseparable from the individual destiny. They determine what the future holds for the individual. The Yoruba and Ibo of Nigeria called this *ori* and *chi* respectively.

Another spirit, which may be the fifth category, is called diviner spirit. It is generally believed that African traditional priest receive revelation from such spirits. Such spirit teaches the diviner medicine. These spirits teaches diagnostic and healing. It is strongly believed that all these spirits are created by God and, in way, messengers of God. God uses them to punish, to deliver, and to bless human beings.

Various usages of Ruach in the Old Testament.

Ruach as wind

The writers of the Old Testament for some important reasons made a meteorological use of the term *ruach*. It does not actually mean any kind of air or wind, but an air in motion. In such usages, the *ruach* in Genesis 1:2 moves over the water; in Isaiah 7:2 the trees shake before the *ruach*. In Genesis 3:8 the *ruach* of the day is the cool of the

Spirit in the OT and in Africa

day. In Exodus 10:13, the east wind brings locusts and blows a strong sea wind into the Sea of Reed. In Exodus 14:21 a powerful cast wind dry the Sea of Reed. In Numbers 11:31, this *ruach* brings quails with it. God made a wind blow over the earth and the flood subsided (Genesis 8:1).

In some cases *ruach* as wind is parallel to the use of *basar* as "weak" and "feeble". It has been discussed previously under *basar* that although it basically means flesh, it is also used to refer to human weakness (Psalms 56:4, Jeremiah 17:5-7).

In the above, they refer to *ruach*, "wind" as mere nothingness (see also Psalms 62:9, 4:4, Ecc. 1:2). The similarity mentioned above however, does not mean that there is no sharp contrast between *basar* and *ruach*. The *ruach* as a strong divine instrument from Yahweh (the *ruach* breaks forth with a deluge of rain with hail Ex.13:13), stands in contrast to *basar* as weakness. *Ruach* as a wind always a mighty phenomenon standing at Yahweh's disposal, is quite distinctive from *basar*.[26]

As discussed above, strong winds contain God's spirit. Sometimes, in African religion, it is regarded as expression of God's anger and punishment. It could be a means of delivering people in danger. In African stories, many important people have been said to have been rescued by wind from danger of motor accident, drowning and other dangers.

Ruach as Breath

The word *ruach* as it is used by some of the Old Testament writers can be synonymous to *nesama* (breath). This literally refers to the wind blown from the nostris. In this case "Thus says Yahweh" who created and formed *ruach*, *Yasar* in people (Zech. 12:1). *Ruach* is not present in idols or stone because they have no breath. The noun *nesama* occurs very rarely to express Psychical realities. It occurs as a collective term for all living creatures and is synonymous to *kol nephesh*, (all souls) and *kol-ruach* (all

Spirit in the OT and in Africa

spirit).

The use of *nesamas*, God,s own breath, shares with ruach the signification of God's life-giving power in creation (Gen. 2:7, 7:22, Isa. 42:5, Job 26:4), and also of the destructive breath of God's divine anger (11 Sam. 22:16; Isa. 30:33, Job 4:9). In the above sense, *sesame is* used as a poetic expression synonymous to *ruach*. They are both used as *ruach hayed* and *nesama hayed* (spirit of life and breath of life respectively).[27]

In Ezekiel 37:6-14, the bones never became life until Yahweh puts his *ruach*. In Ecclesiastes 12:7, when one dies, his *ruach* (breath) returns to God who gave it. It is also noticeable to talk about the moving out and the coming in of *ruach* as in *nephesh* (Job. 12:10). In *nephesh* we see the organ of breathing and the process of breathing itself together, but in *ruach* we see the wind proceeding from Yahweh and returning to him which constituted man's breath of life (Job 34:14).[28] If he should take back his *ruach* to himself, and gather to himself his breath, all flesh would perish together, and man would return to dust (Job. 34:14-15). The image of the new Carmel in Jeremiah 2:24 reflects how *ruach* as a breath and *nephesh* as the organ of breath belong together Job 19:17 says, that his *ruach* is repulsive to his wife and that he smells loathsome to his son. *Ruach* as wind is synonymous to *nesama*, and *nephesh* for it is stated that all life and death depend on *ruach*.

In one version of Yoruba story of creation, *Olodumare* (the Supreme God) created human being and gave somebody else the task of attaching all parts of the body to human being, but Olodumare alone was the only person who gave his breathe (also called *emi*). That *emi* belongs to God alone in Yoruba religious tradition. He is the only one who can give it.

Ruach as vital Power[29]

What I have discovered so far reveals that *ruach* as breath

Spirit in the OT and in Africa

is inseparable from *ruach* of Yahweh (Job 34:14; Psalm 104:29). What we mean by *ruach* as vital power is *ruach* of Yahweh, which is more than ordinary enlivening "wind" which becomes the breath of man. It means the power that moves creation. Psalm 33:6 says, "By the word of the Lord the heavens were made and all their host by the *ruach* of this mouth." In the above, *ruach* is synonymous to "word" and both proceed from the mouth. It should be translated "word.". Yahweh's breath means creative power of life. Yahweh's *ruach* determines man's life span (Gen. 6:4) because it is a life-giving power. Natural forces are under the control of the *ruach* of Yahweh. "At the *ruach* (translated blast) of thy nostrils the waters piled up, the floods stood up in hill" (Exodus 15:8). This vital power of Yahweh when it descended on judges, kings and prophets, power and authority resulted

Othniel went to battle and saved Israel (Jg. 3: 10). Samson tore a lion into pieces (Jg. 14:16). The *ruach* of Yahweh was upon Saul, and he became another man (I Sam. 10: 6). This vital power of *ruach* of Yahweh produced special, abilities to prophesy. In Numbers 24:2, Balaam prophesized. The presence of this *ruach* also gives wisdom and understanding. When Pharaoh looked for a man who has the *ruach* of God in him, he meant someone with extraordinary wisdom in the sense of economic policy (Genesis 41: 33:39). Here *ruach* should be translated wisdom, with Yahweh's *ruach* there should be authority (Ez. 11:15; 1:3 and Isaiah 42: 1).

Ruach as Independent Spirit

The word *ruach* may refer to an invisible independent being. This may be, or it may not necessarily be Yahweh's spirit. This may be a form of supernatural angelic being."[30] According to II Kings 19:7, he would put his spirit in him (the King of Assyria) so that he will hear a rumor and return to his own land. We read of the false *ruach* sent by Yahweh, which deluded the Prophets of Ahab (I Kings 22:21). This *ruach* is like assembly of powers to be

Spirit in the OT and in Africa

distributed to different places to perform several functions.[31] God may allow his *ruach* to appear in form of *ruhot* "wind" (Psalms 104:4) and as "fire" (I Kings 19:11-12). The function of this may be revelatory as in Job 4:16 and Zech. 1:9,19.

Satan is the greatest accusing spirit (I Kings 22:21). Joshua's leadership when he succeeded Moses, was also under the appeal to the one who is the God of "vital spirit," (*ruhot*) of all flesh (Numb. 27:16, 16:22). From what has been said above, it is necessary to know that, the *ruach* as a vital power of every man, as authority and as independent being is at God's disposal.[32]

Ruach as feeling

In our previous discussion, I have mentioned that the *nephesh* as one of the psychological terms can refer to desire, that vital longing, desiring, striving or yearning. We have also stated that *leb* can equally mean feelings and wish from the heart. So also *ruach* can mean feelings. This further authenticates the fluidity or fluctuation of these terms. This is also due to the concept of cooperate personality in the Hebrew thought of man.

It is even difficult to have any clear-cut dichotomy from *ruach* as "breath" and *ruach* as the "organ of knowledge, understanding, judgment and feelings. As we examine breath, we discover that the rise and fall of breath may correspond with his feelings. That is the reason why when the Queen of Sheba saw the wisdom of Solomon, there was no more *ruach* in her (I Kings 10:5). This means that her breath stopped and she lost her consciousness.[33] Attitude of mind can demonstrate one's *ruach*. When Eliphaz accused Job that he had turned his *ruach* against God, he was talking about his mind and attitude to God (Job 15:13). *Ruach* here can mean feeling. Jezebel also noticed that Ahab's *ruach* had turned away and he refused to eat, she meant that he was "ill humoured"(I. Kings 21:4). Yahweh hardened Sihon's *ruach*, so that he behaved flexibly (Dent. 2:30). Eccl. 7:8 talks about the patient and the proud *ruach*. *Ruach* can also mean one's spiritual disposition Prov. 18:14). When it is stated in Isaiah 19:14, Yahweh brought "a spirit of confusion" among the princes of Egypt, he meant a confusing state of mind. *Ruach* in this case can be translated feeling.

Ruach as the Will of Man

Just as *leb* can mean "will" or "decision" of a man, so also *ruach* can refer to human will. The *leb* which means "will" has been discussed previously. I shall now discuss several occasions when *ruach* means will. When Ezra spoke of the exile whose *ruach* God stirred up to go back to Jerusalem to rebuild it, he was talking about their will (Ez.1 1:5). Jer. 51. 11 talked about the *ruach* to destroy and to build by the Kings of Medes. This means the will to destroy and rebuild Babylon. Hosea accused Israel of the *ruach* of harlotry (Hos. 4:2). In several other passages, *ruach* means the will of man, which God gave, or the will of man, which comes from other sources. Num. 14:34, Ps. 51, Ez. 11: 19, 36:26 are few of these places where *ruach* can mean will. In the above places, *ruach* can therefore be translated "will" instead of "spirit."

Conclusion

What I have been saying is that *Ruach* is one of the most important biblical terms in the Old Testament. Yet despite its importance, it is one of the most mistranslated terms in the Old Testament. In most cases, it has been translated "spirit" where it should have been translated wisdom, feelings, will, breath, word, power or wing.

Unfortunately, the translations of this term "spirit" in most of the Bible translation to African languages follow this same error in English translation. This is especially true in the translation of the Bible into the three major languages of Nigeria (Yoruba, Hausa and Ibo). This writer believes that there is a need for a revision of the present translation so that African translators do not follow the

English version verbatim. One word can really make a difference in the meaning of some Bible passages. I hope that a day will come when the best African biblical scholars will gather together and strive towards having a perfect African translation or version of the Bible that may be English or any of the most famous African languages.[34]

[1] This article was originally published in the Bulletin of Biblical Studies, University of Athens.

[2] H. Wheeler Robinson, "Hebrew Psychology," in *The People and the book* edited by Arthur S. Peake (Oxford: Claredon Press, 1925), 353.

[3] Ibid.
[4] Edmond Jacob, *Theology of the Old Testament*, Trans. Arthur W. Heathcote and Philip J. Allcorck, New York: Harper and Brothers Publishers, 1958

[5] Robinson, 354.
[6] Ibid.,
[7] Ibid., 366.
[8] Ibid. Hans Walter Wolff, *Anthropology of the Old Testament* (Philadelphia Fortress Press, 1981), 157.

[9] Hans Walter Wolff, *Anthropology of the Old Testament* (Philadelphia Fortress Press, 1981), 157.
[10] Gerhard Von Rad, *Old Testament Theology* Vol. 2, trans. DMG Stalker (New York: Harper and Row Publishers, 1962-1965), 152-153.

[11] Ibid. ,11. See also Prov. 10:3, Jere. 31:12, 25, Prov. 27:7 Num. 21.5.

[12] See also Prov. 16:26, Hosea 4:8.
[13] Wolff, 26.
[14] Ibid.,
[15] John Pederson, *Israel: Its Life and Culture* (London: Oxford University Press, 1926) Vol. 1, 171. Pederson went as far as saying that the body is the soul in its outward form.

[16] Wolff, 26.
[17] Ibid., 31.
[18] *Theological Word Book of the Old Testament*, 218.

[19] Ibid.

[20] Wolff, p. 44.

[21] Brown, Driver and Briggs, A *Hebrew-English Lexicon of the Old Testament* (Oxford: Claredon Press, Reprinted 1977) 924. R. Hams, G.L. Archer, B.K. Waitke, *Theological Wordbook of the Old Testament* (Chicago Mooddy Press, 1981), 218.

[22] Wolff, 32.

[23] Wolff quoting D. Lys, 32.

[24] Wolff, 32.
[25] Wolff, 32. quoting Lys.
[26] Ibid., 33.
[27] Eichrodt, 142.
[28] wolff, 33.
[29] Ibid.
[30] R.L Hals et. al. *Theological Wordbook*, 2133.
[31] Wolff., 36.
[32] Ibid.
[33] Ibid.
[34] This paper was originally presented at the conference of the Nigerian Association for Biblical Studies, Ibadan, Nigeria in October 4-7, 1989. Bulletin of Biblical Studies, University of Athens, Greece, later published it.

SUFFERING IN THE OLD TESTAMENT AND IN AFRICAN CONTEXT[1]

Introduction

The problem of suffering is a problem that cannot be ignored in human existence. No problem that is more common to human and is a more serious threat to faith like the problem of human suffering. The problem is especially serious for both Christianity and Judaism. In both the Old and the New Testament, it appears as if the higher one's concept of God is, the greater this problem becomes. It makes one ask, why, God? If God is a personal God, and the Creator who is all-powerful, just, and in control of this universe, why is the problem of suffering?

The Old Testament gives us the most comprehensive survey of the problem of suffering as far as theistic religion is concerned. This problem later became central in the religion of Israel. According to the prophetic interpretation of the laws of Yahweh, if men did justice, loved and walked humbly before God, they are expected to prosper. Thus, when Judah was struck by Sennacherib, Isaiah said to his countrymen, "Come now, let us reason together, says the Lord: though your sins are like crimson, they shall become like wool. If you are willing and obedient ' you shall eat the good of the land; but if you refuse and rebel ye shall be devoured by sword; for the mouth of the Lord has spoken" (Isa. 1:18-19). Josianic reformation meant that Judah was righteous and as a result, must be prosperous. But that proved contradictory by a series of tragedies during the destruction of Jerusalem. The faith of Israel was clearly directed toward a personal, active and divine Being who is believed to be the Creator, the controller of history, the omniscient and omnipresent God. If Israel was the people of Yahweh, and all power was his, why should Israel suffer? Why is Yahweh so indifferent to the suffering of the righteous, and the triumph of the godless oppressors?

The answers to these problems have never been a simple one. The Old Testament offers no one satisfactory solution, but several. This section of this book is a discussion of several solutions that the Old Testament has offered. It considered suffering as retributive, disciplinary, and educational, probational, revelational, redemptive, and eschatological. In the following pages, more elaboration will be given to the above-mentioned solutions to suffering.

Suffering as Retributive

It appears that biblical writers are not actually interested in seeking the origin of suffering. Their main concern was the reason and the purpose of it. In the earliest state of the Hebrew faith, suffering was interpreted as a divine punishment for sin.[2] This retributive principle of suffering is basic to the Old Testament. This retributive principle is very common in the Pentateuch. This principle is seen in the Genesis account of God's righteous judgment upon the disobedient man (Gen. 3:16-19). In the book of Exodus, the Lord punished the Egyptians with plaques because of Pharaoh's wickedness (Exod 9). Leviticus lays much emphasis on the consequences of breaking the Lord's commandments.[3]

> But if ye will not hearken unto me, and will not do all these commandments; And if ye shall despise my statutes, or if your soul abhor my judgments, so that ye will not do all my commandments but that ye break my

covenant: I also will do this unto you; I will even appoint over you terror, consumption, and the burning plague, that shall consume the eyes, and cause sorrow of heart: and ye shall sow your seed in vain for your enemies shall eat it. And I will set my face against you and ye shall be slain before your enemies: they that hate you shall reign over you; and ye shall flee when none pursueth you (Lev: 26:14-17).

In the book of Numbers, Miriam became leprous when she and Aaron spoke against Moses because he married the African woman (Numbers 12: 1-10). The book of Deuteronomy gathers up the teaching of the eighth century prophets by saying:

"The Lord shall send upon thee cursing, vexation, and rebuke in all that thou settest thine hand unto for to do until thou be destroyed, and until thou perish quickly; because of the wickedness of their doings, whereby thou has forsaken me. The Lord shall make the pestilence cleave unto thee until he hath consumed thee from off the land, whither thou goest to possess it" (Deut. 28:20-21).

Almost every chapter of the writings of the prophets illustrates the interpretation of suffering as the just recompense and reward of sin, its necessary accompaniment in the moral government of the world by Yahweh.[4] In Amos in particular, there was an emphasis on a series of contemporary cases of sufferings in the form of famine, drought, the destruction of the harvest, pestilence, defeat in battle and earthquake, as a warning penalties preparatory of Yahweh's final judgment on sin.[5] Amos also sees suffering as retributive in the case of pagan nations (Amos 1:3-15, 2:13). According to the prophet Hosea, Yahweh declares, "I will punish them form their ways, and will reward them their doings. For they shall eat, and not have enough. They shall commit whoredom, and shall not increase: because they have left off to take heed to the Lord" (Hosea 4:9). Israel hath cast off that which is good. The enemy shall pursue him (8:3); Isaiah asks, "Why

Suffering in the OT and in African Context

should ye be striken any more?" (Isa. 1:5). He continues, "Woe unto the wicked. It shall be ill with him for the reward of his hands shall be given him" (Isa. 3:11). The Prophet Micah has this to say about the rulers of Israel: "They build up Zion with blood and Jerusalem with iniquity. Therefore shall Zion for your sake be plowed as a field, and Jerusalem shall become heaps and the mountain of the house as high places of the foresto." (Micah 3:10,12). Haggai asserts that the sufferings of the returned exiles are due to delay in rebuilding of the Temple. (Haggai 1:57).

The Psalmist maintains with strong confidence that destruction of the wicked is retributive (Psalm 37). That suffering is a divine judgment upon sin is fundamental to the Old Testament teaching can also be seen in the wisdom literature. The book of Job in its most striking literary expression illustrates this principle as an orthodox doctrine of Israel. Job's three friends firmly hold that great suffering is to be explained by great sinfulness, that is why much of his friend's speeches consist of descriptions of God's judgment on the wicked.

They started from the general basic belief that Yahweh; the Omnipotent God must be righteous. What he does must be right without question because he can never pervert justice. Therefore, there is no way Job can be righteous before God and suffer like he did. They urged him to turn to God because they were convinced that job's suffering must be caused by sin, Thus in the Old Testament sin and punishment go together just as sin and guilt do. The three terms are involved in each other. Indeed the three ideas were so intimately related to each other in the Hebrew thought that the same words were used to express them all.

In African religious tradition, there is a strong belief that suffering is retributive. That is why most parents tell stories to their children daily to teach them that suffering is retributive. These types of stories are many in Africa. Africans teach their children not only through stories, but also through proverbs and sayings concerning retribution. I remember the common Yoruba proverb, which says: *Eni ba nyole da ibi a maa yoo se.* It literally means that any person who does evil in secret will experience evil in secret. It teaches that evil people should watch out because an evil person cannot go unpunished because the Supreme Being is aware of all secret evil performed everywhere. My late mother used to say in Iyagba language that *Olorun ti gboro e ti mehin rin, nitoripe aropile i gun ni. Literally it means that the god of today does not treck, but flies in aeroplane.* It is an expression to show that our modern God does not waste time in revenging. The Yoruba people of Nigeria are quick to say that this proverb when offended: *Fi ja fun Olorun ja fowo leran.* It means do not revenge by yourself. Leave everything to God who is a God of vengeance. This saying corresponds with the biblical saying, "Recompense to no man evil for evil...Vengeance is mine, I will repay, saith the Lord" (Rom. 12:17,19). Such proverb is said when someone who has more power and authority offends.

Suffering as Divine Discipline

The view that suffering is disciplinary is closely related to the retributive view because it sees, the affliction of the - people as God's visitation for some reason other than punishment.[6]The purpose of this visitation is disciplinary and educational. It is for the sake of bringing them back to himself. If God really loves his children, he should discipline them.

The Hebrew word *Yasar* has the basic meaning of learning or teaching a lesson. This lesson may be learned in three ways. First, through experience of suffering; second through accepting verbal instruction without any sufferings; and third, through observing a given situation. The idea of disciplinary suffering is used as a connotation of *Y a s a r* thirty-three times in twenty verses, out of ninety-two. It is used 18 times. in seventeen verses in the prophets, five times in four verses in Leviticus and Deuteronomy, eight times in seven verses in the Psalms, and three verses in Job and Proverbs,[7] *Y a s a r* is used to

Suffering in the OT and in African Context

indicate a divine disciplinary suffering inflicted upon a nation twenty times in twenty-two verses and eight times in eight verses to indicate a disciplinary suffering upon the individual.

The Prophet Jeremiah is the most popular preacher of suffering as disciplinary. Prophet Jeremiah uses the root *M u s a r* and *Y a s a r* to express discipline. The root *Ya s a r* occurs nine times in eight verses of authentic Jeremianic materials.[8] Five of these verses have the connotation of God teaching a lesson by afflicting and experiencing suffering when the use of *M u s a r* is employed (Jer. 2:30, 5:3, 2:191, 30:14, 31:18).[9] Twice the word *Musar* conveys the meaning of the lesson imparted through warnings (7:28-6:18) and once conveys lesson by observation (2:30).

Several events, which the prophet Jeremiah witnessed before and after his commission, helped him to formulate his messages where the false security of Jerusalem was assumed. After the withdrawal of Sennacherib (70/13CE) there was a shift from Yahwistic religion during the reign of Manasseh. The discovery of the law book in 621 and its, use (3: 10 ' 8:8-9), the rise of the new Babylonian empire , the destruction of Nineveh in 612, the sudden death of Josiah at Megiddo in 608, the defeat of Pharaoh Necco in 605, by Nebuchadnezzar, and finally, the follies of Josiah's heirs in Jerusalem (Jer. 22:8)[10] led the prophet to reach the conclusion that the defeat and downfall of Judah, the destruction of Jerusalem and the exile of the people were inevitable. Jeremiah refers to the coming destruction when he says, "Your evil will discipline you and your apostates will reprove you." (Jer. 2:19). God must pluck up, break, destroy, and overthrow (1: 10). The people had failed to heed the message of Jeremiah. They have failed to repent. In other words, they have failed to have *d a'a t Eloh i m.* (The knowledge of God). The only alternative left to bring them to God was discipline in form of captivity. Therefore, the purpose of the coming suffering is to bring repentance and *d a 'a t El o h im.* The suffering of Jeremiah himself has the purpose of

Suffering in the OT and in African Context

bringing him closer to God. Suffering is therefore, regarded as an act of love to bring in the children of Israel to a new covenantal relationship. The book of Isaiah chapter 9 also expressed the idea of suffering as disciplinary. It says for all this his anger is not turned away, but his hand is stretched out still. Why has the Lord's anger not turned away? The answer is in verse 12. The wrath of God was meant to him, but "The people have not returned to him who smote them nor have they sought the Lord of hosts." (9:12).

According to Second Isaiah 42:25, the Lord has given Jacob to spoilers and Israel to robbers, but they have not returned to him so he must lead them and guide them himself. Out of this comes the great solution message of the Second Isaiah. In Ezekiel 16:27-28 and 23:18-20, the Lord's anger and wrath against the people for playing harlot with their neighbors and forgetting him was supposed to have the effect of stopping their harlotry and, by implication, returning to. God.[11]

There are references in Amos to divine wrath of God as disciplinary (Amos 2:9-11 and 9:7). The action in these passages became favorable to the people. But in Amos 4:6-11, the disasters (famine-, drought, crop failure, pestilence and destruction by fire) had the purpose of making the people return to the Lord. But alas! they did not return unto me, says the Lord.

The book of Haggai 2:17 is similar to the thought of Amos 4 and Isaiah 9. "I smote for you all the work of your hands with blight, mildew and nail, yet you did not return to me says the Lord."

The passage of Zachariah referring to the calamity of 586 says that the Lord's curses fell upon the fathers and they repented. Psalm 78 contains the ideas that God's anger caused 'the people to repent.

In both Leviticus 26 and Deuteronomy, we have consequences of obedience and disobedience. If, in spite of these sufferings, the people do not hearken to God, their leadership will increase sevenfold. In Deuteronomy 8:5 the purpose of the people's afflictions during the forty-year's wandering in the wilderness was to test them to see what was in their heart and whether or not they would keep God's commandments. God has given them manna to teach them that man does not live by bread alone.

Hosea used *Y a s a r* in these passages: 5:2, 7:12, and 10:10 which carry with them the idea of divine discipline. The exact expressions referring to divine discipline is only found in Zephariah 3:2 and 7.

The third chapter of Lamentation expresses the idea of afflictions from God as good and purposeful. In the Wisdom literature, the word for chastening *M u s a r* is frequently used. Proverb 3:2 says, "My son, despise not the chastening of the Lord; neither be weary of his reproof." He says about the man chastening with pain who is brought very near to death in his suffering, that this suffering, interpreted to him by an angelic messenger of God, may move him to the humble penitence which is the condition of recovery, so that finally the sufferer restored to health, will sing God's praise. Eliphaz reminds Job that "Happy is the man whom God correcteth: Therefore, despise not thou the chastening of the Almighty" (Job 5:17).

The idea that suffering may be a way realize he needs to seek repentance is also clear among African people. The Yoruba people of Nigeria are quick to express this in their proverbs: *Bi Olorun ba nse rere, a lo nse ibi.* If God is doing something good for us, we think he is doing evil. The understanding is that the suffering may be a way to correct the bad things we are doing. It is a way of bringing us to repentance. This proverb also expresses the idea that suffering may be revelational. This will be discussed later under suffering as revelational.

Suffering as Probationary and Evidential

The third solution to suffering in the Old Testament is that suffering is temporary. Prophet Habakkuk is a classic illustration of this probationary view. Prophet Habakkuk looking out from his watchtower, upon this contemporary world, sees nothing but violence, oppression, and tyranny. Those people who were involved in these wicked things were apparently successful. The question in the prophet's mind as he comes to argue with God's justice, is how God can honor a wicked nation, the Chaldeans, above a divinely appointed one. The prophet cries out and asks God, "Wherefore lookest thou upon them that deal treacherously, and holdest thy peace when the wicked swalloweth up the man that is more righteous than he? (Heb. 1: 13). The answer, which the prophet receives, is that the present condition is temporary. The righteous must therefore be patient waiting for the retributive principle to be manifested. This patience involves some quality of faithfulness of the righteous man. "The just shall live by his faithfulness" (Heb. 2:4). Since the world is evil, the godly must wait for the disposition of wickedness and the righteousness, which is sure to come. In this probational period man's faith is submitted to a rigid test which determines the real character of his faith.'[12] A similar solution to the question is also illustrated in Malachi 2:17 and 3:14-18. The author of Malachi faces the problem of people saying that "Everyone that doeth evil is good in the sight of Yahweh and he delighted in them... it is vain to serve God... yea, they that work wickedness are built up." The answer given to that is that, the righteous has their names written in the book of remembrance against that day of judgment when one shall discern between the righteous and the wicked and between those who serve God and those who serve him not.

In Psalm 37, the man who is perplexed by the similar problem is bidden. "Fret not thyself because of evil-doers, neither be envious against the workers of iniquity. Trust in the Lord and do good; so shall thou dwell in the land and verily thou shalt be fed." The writer continues his admonition that the righteous should wait for the vindications of Yahweh's government of the world.

B. Davidson sees the entire book of Job to be teaching the probational view of suffering.[13] Earlier the Hebrew outlook on shoel afforded no prospect beyond the grave. But later the pressure of the problem of suffering of the righteous and the apparent prosperity of the wicked compelled some people to ask the question. Since our life in this world is limited, how can the righteous be rewarded? Can there be a life beyond death, which will compensate for the inadequate retribution of this life? The two principal teachings of immorality in Psalm and Job are direct outcome of the problem of suffering. The two important assertions of resurrection found in Isaiah 26:19 and Daniel 12:2 are as a result of a demand for an answer to the problem of suffering.[14] It led them to affirm that there must be another life, supernaturally restored, though still to be lived on this earth. Thus, the martyred to whom apocalyptic writers refer will come back to life. The faithful in the Maccabean persecution who died during the persecution will similarly be raised to receive their permanent reward while the wicked will be raised to receive their punishment.

Suffering as Revelational

The fourth solution to suffering is that suffering can be revelational. This view refers to "physical evil as the occasion of man's entry into a fuller knowledge of God."[15] The Old Testament no doubt confirms the fact that many have found the true glory of God in suffering. This can be seen in the way in which suffering enables the prophetic consciousness to enter into a deeper knowledge of God and his relation to man. The most striking example is the sufferings of Israel as a nation and the experience of the Prophet Hosea. It is evident that Israel actually reached her highest concept of God during her greatest suffering. The Exodus experience and the captivity are classic examples of the time of revelation. The tragedy of the domestic life of the Prophet Hosea, with his relationship to his people and the sufferings of the Prophet open his mind to see the love of Yahweh, which persists against all the infidelity of his people (Hosea 1:8-11). This suffering in the book of Hosea covers not only the disobedience of Israel to her divine husband, but also the absolute truth that the patience and the love of Yahweh will definitely win back his people at all cost. Such advance knowledge of God would have been probably impossible at the age of Israel's history, if it were not for the context of Hosea's personal experience, through which God was revealed to him.[16]

Another important example of deeper revelation as a result of suffering can be seen in the life experience of a Prophet who most closely resembles Hosea in temperament and clearly shows his influence Jeremiah. Jeremiah experienced both physical and spiritual sufferings, which enables him to know God and have unwavering courage to stand for him. Jeremiah wit
nessed several national calamities as noted previously in this essay.[17] Jeremiah's first message was against the temple the center of the religious institution, and the center of the priests and - Prophet's livelihood. The result was an arrest and banishment from the temple. Because he was banned from the temple, Jeremiah began to write his message down so that it could be read to the people.

But at last, King Jehoiakim tore the written scroll containing his message to pieces. Jeremiah's preaching of submission to the Babylonians and his condemnation of Judah's alliance with foreign nations put him to trouble with the political authority. The result was another arrest again by Pashour. He was beaten and thrown into the stock. Jeremiah was opposed dramatically and vehemently by the false prophets. Unfortunately, the authorities believed the false prophets message instead of Jeremiah's. The priests and the officers of Zedekiah attempted to take Jeremiah's life. He was thrown to a cistern until he was delivered by Ebed - Melech. Jeremiah and Baruch were later forced to go to Egypt after the assasination of Gedaliah. Jeremiah continued his prophecy and propably died there.

No doubt, Jeremiah's suffering and his "isolation from men threw him the more upon God and issued a new type of personal religion with far reaching consequences." His suffering brought him closer to God. Jeremiah, in deep reflection, after facing God in his deepest despair, feels him in his deepest humility. Because Jeremiah has experienced, in a sense, God's own harsh discipline, he rises from depths with a new quality and a new sense of values.[18] Having experienced the *d a 'a t E I o h im* he was able to proclaim a new covenant and a new relationship between God and Israel.

Job's experience can be regarded as revelational also. Job rejects all the explanation, of his suffering given by his three friends as inadequate. He rejects the popular Hebrew concept of suffering as retributive and disciplinary as offered by Elphaz and Elihu. The very position reached by job himself after a lot of struggle is that it is possible to see, not darkness, but light in suffering. He sees the vision of God, which releases him from his problem of suffering. He declares: "I have heard thee by the hearing of the ear, but now mine eye seeth thee. Wherefore, I abhor myself and repent in dust and ashes (Job 42:5-6)."

As promised above that the Yoruba proverbs which says, *Bi Olorun ba nse rere, a lo nse ibi* expresses the perfect idea that God's work is incomprehensible. At times he uses suffering to reveal himself to us. He reveals to us something we do not know because of our limited knowledge during the period of suffering.

Suffering as Redemptive

The redemptive solutions to suffering in the Old Testament is closely related to two theories. (1) that physical evil may be redemptive when suffered for others (2) and it may also be redemptive in the sense that it can achieve victory in spite of the suffering. The Old Testament reaches its deepest solution to the problem of the suffering of the righteous in the thought that the innocent may suffer for others.[19] "This is the idea incarnated in the figure of the suffering Servant of Yahweh, the noblest creation of Old Testament religion." The Suffering Servant of Yahweh passages in the Second Isaiah 40-55 form the chief illustration of the concept that suffering can be sacrificial.[20]

In attempting to identify this Servant of Yahweh, several possibilities have been suggested by critics.[21] This identification falls into two classifications - group and individual. This Servant of Yahweh is regarded as the nation of Israel as a group, and both Israel and individual. As an individual, this Servant has been identified with Zerubbabel, Jehoiakim, Moses, Jeremiah, Unnamed teachers of the Torah, the Ethiopian Eunuch, the dying, and resurrected god of vegetation, and Jesus Christ -the Messiah.

The view that the Suffering Servant of Yahweh represents Israel nation is very appealing and, of course, accepted. Thus, the fifty-third chapter of Isaiah can be regarded as a philosophy of the sufferings of the nation in their national pride and religious faith. Several times Israel is described as Yahweh's Servant in such phrases as Thou Israel and my servant Jacob whom I have chosen. So Israel's mission to the heathen is the leading idea in the Second Isaiah. Israel's election to be Yahweh's Servant should be interpreted in the light of this mission to the heathen."[22]Her sufferings in exile should therefore be interpreted as a guilt offering for the nation of the world, which will not only move them to repentance, but also make for them a sacrificial means of approach to God, and the death of the nations, would be followed by a glorious majestic resurrection.[23] This is to be accomplished through the glorious restoration of Israel, at which Kings and Princes shall rise and worship.

Suffering as Eschatological

The final solution to suffering sees the answer beyond the present conflict.[24] It is based on a faith that in the time of great darkness, pain and fear God will suddenly reveal himself in order, to save and reward his own because the righteous. God will not leave his righteous people who have suffered persecution unrewarded.

Isaiah 24-27 is, one of the important earliest Old Testament texts for eschatological solution to suffering. Here the author described a universal judgment on the nations for bloodshed and oppression. This judgment involves Yahweh's punishment of the wicked people (empires) who oppressed the righteous, and the resurrection of the people of Yahweh.

The book of Daniel Chapter 7-12 seems to be a development of the concept found earlier in Isaiah 24-27.[25] This book came up to encourage the Jews in the terrible persecution they were going through for their loyalty to the religion during the time of Antiochus Epiphanes (165 A.D.).

There was to be an unprecedented tribulation for the punishment of the wicked, but the righteous Jews who were presently undergoing persecution would be delivered. Resurrection will also take place.

> And many of them that sleep in the dust of the earth shall awake, some to everlasting life, and some to shame and everlasting punishment contempt. And they that are wise shall shine as the brightness of the firmament and they that turn many to righteousness as the stars forever and ever (Dan. 12:2-3).

The passage quoted above came out of a historical situation. What actually was working in the mind of the author was the heroic constancy to God that was displayed by the martyrs. What will be their fate when Israel triumph and God's Kingdom is set up on earth? The answer is "they must be raised from the dead to share in his glories."

Psalm 58,73 and 82 also presented an eschatological solution to suffering. The misgovernment of the angelic guardians of the nations is doomed to punishment. 73 are eschatological in the sense that the future state of the wicked is offered as a solution to the problem of the prosperity of those who defy God.

Job 19:23-29 presents a perfect example of an eschatological solution to suffering. Job was convinced that death does not close the issue of suffering.

> Oh that my words were written! Oh that they were graven with an iron pen and lead in the rock forever! For I know that my redeemer liveth, and that he shall stand at the latter day upon the earth; And though my skin worms destroy this body yet in my flesh shall I see God. Whom, I shall see for myself, and mine eyes shall behold, and not another; though my reins be consumed within me (Job 19:23-27).

No doubt, this Hebrew form of belief in resurrection as a solution to suffering of the righteous influenced the literature of the later Judaism, Christianity, and Islam. An example is a famous passage from the Wisdom of Solomon:

> The soul of the righteous are in the hand of God, And no torment shall touch them. In the eyes of the foolish they seemed to have died; And their departure was accounted to be their hurt, And their journeying away from us to be their ruin: But they are in peace. For even if in the sight of men they be punished, Their hope is full of immortality; And having borne a little chastening, they shall receive great good; Because God made trial of them and found them worthy of Himself. As gold in the furnace He proved them. And as a whole burnt offering He accepted them (Wise of Solo 3:1-6).

Conclusion

In conclusion, I must say that the retributive, disciplinary and probational, revelational, redemptive, and eschatological solution to suffering in the Old Testament, though important, is not a complete answer to the problems of suffering. The Bible confesses the fact that the solution to suffering is a mystery. What one needs to know that God has a sovereign purpose with human being and history. It is therefore impossible to judge this very purpose fully and rightly in a circumstance.

Any theoretical solution to suffering is practically

impossible and, of course, unnecessary. Thus the solution to suffering is practical and is faith, which must prevail in all circumstances. The book of Job is an example of the text which teaches that suffering is still a mystery.

All these Old Testament solutions to the problem of suffering are also carried to the New Testament. There are abundant New Testament evidences to retributive (Jn. 9:13,'Lk. -13:.1-5), disciplinary (Heb. 2:10, 5:8-9, Rom. 5:3-5), probationary (Matt. 1.0:24, Jn. 15:18-21, 1 Cor. 12:26), revelational (I Pet. 3:17), eschatological (Matt. 24:13, Rom. 8:18), and mysterious solution (Lk. 23:46) to suffering.

The pessimism of Ecclesiastics is noteworthy before the end of this section. This book seems exceptional in its approach to suffering. There is no evidence of retribution and life beyond the grave.

Endnotes

[1] "Suffering in the Old Testament," *Bulletin of Biblical studies*, Vol.8 (Jan. - June, 1989), University of Athens, 30-42.

[2] Wheeler Robinson, *Suffering Human and Divine* (New York: The Macmillan Comp. 1939), 3.

[3] Ibid., 31-32.
[4] O.A Piper, *Interpreters' Dictionary of the Bible* (IDB), vol.5 A.Burttrick ed. (Nashville: Abingdon Press, 1962),451.
[5] Gordon Clinard, "Biblical Preaching on Suffering," *Southwestern Journal of Theology*, (April 1963), 33-41.
[6] Gordon Clinard, "Biblical Preaching on Suffering," *Southwestern Journal of Theology* (SWJTH), April 1959, 20
[7] Jim Sanders, "Suffering as Divine Discipline in the Old Testament and Post Biblical Judiasm," *Colgate Rochester Divinity School Bulletin*, (1955) 42.

[8] Scholarship generally see Jer. 10:1-16, 23-25, 17:19-27, as secondary, 2:19, 30, 5:3, 7:28, 30:1431:18, and 35:13, are generally regarded as genuine Jeremanic passages. Jim Sanders, "Suffering as Divine Discipline in the Old Testament," 11, 17.

9 Ibid.46.
10 Ibid. 47.
11 Ibid., 81.
12 Gordon Clinard, "Biblical Preaching on Suffering," *SWJTH, (1959), 21.*
13 A.B Davidson, *Theoogy of the Old Testament* (Edinburgh: T& T Clark, 1949), 286.
14 Gordon Clinard, "Biblical Preacing on Suffering," *SWJTH* (April 1959), 21.
15 Ibid.
16 H. Wheeler Robinson, *Suffering Human and Divine*, 42-43.
17 Jeremiah witnessed the false security of Jerusalem as assumed after the withdrawal of Sennacherib in 701, the drift from Yahwistic religion during the reign of Mannasseh, the discovery of the law book in 621, the rise of the Babylonian Empire and its destruction pJ Nineveh in 612, the death of Josiah at Meggido in 608 and the defeat Nebuchadnezzar of Pharoah Neco in 605.

18 17. Gordon Clinard, "Biblical Preaching on Suffering," *SWJ TH* (April 1959), 22.
19 H. Wheeler Robinson, *The Religious Ideas of the Old Testament*,

176. See also Gordon Clinard, "Biblical Preaching on Suffering," *SWJTH*, (April 1959), 22.

20 Ibid.176.
21 Robert H. Pfeiffer, *Introduction to the Old Testament*, 459-462.

22 A. S. Peake, *The Problem of Suffering in the Old Testament*(London: Epworth Press, 1947),34.

23 H. Wheeler Robinson, *Suffering Human and Divine*, 44.

24 A. S. Peake, *The Problem of Suffering in the Old Testament*, 109. 24. Ibid.109.

25 Ibid. 109.

SELECTED BIBLIOGRAPHY

Adamo, David Tuesday. *African American Heritage*, 3rdedition completely updated, Eugene, Oregon: Wipf and Stock Publishers, 2001.

_____ Africa and Africans in the Old Testament, San Francisco: Christian University Press, 1998, reprinted by Wipf and Stock Publishers, Oregon, 2001.

_____Africa and Africans in the New Testament. Book manuscript to be published by Judson Press, Valley Forge, PA, 2002.

_____"African Cultural Hermeneutics," in Vernacular Hermeneutics edited by R.S Sugirtharajah. Sheffield: Sheffield Academic Press, 1999.

_____"The Problem of Translating Hebrew Old Testament into Yoruba Language of Nigeria," *The Bible Translator*, Oct. vol. 35 no 4 1984

_____"The Church. in Africa and African Traditional Religious Beliefs and practices", Unpublished Dissertatiorn, 1985 Rel.D.. Indiana Christian University, Indianapolis.

_____ "The Concept of Peace in the Old Testament and in Africa," *The Bible in African Christianity: Essays in Biblical Theology*. Nairobi: Acton Publishers, 1997

_____"Suffering in the Old Testament," *Bulletin of Biblical studies*, Vol.8 (Jan. - June, 1989), University of Athens

_____"Understanding Genesis Creation Account in an African Background" *Caribbean Journal of Religious Studies* (CJRS), Vol. 10, No. 2, (Sept. 1989)

_____"The Images of Cush in the Old Testament: Reflections on African Hermeneutics" in *Interpreting the Old Testament in Africa*. Editors K. Holter, Getui, and Victor Zinkuratired, Peter Lang

Publishing Inc, New York, 2001

_____"The African Wife of Moses: An Examination of Numbers 12:1-9," *Africa Theological Journal* Vol. 18 no 3. (1989) 230-237,

_____"Deuteronomic Conception of God According to Deuteronomy 6:4 in an African Context," *Bible Bhashyam*, (1992), 55-64

_____"The African Wife of Moses: An Examination of Numbers 12:1-9," *Africa Theological Journal* Vol. 18 no 3. (1989) 230-237

_____"The Black Prophet in the Old Testament," *Journal of Arabic and Religious Studies (JARS)*, Vol. 4 (Dec. 1987), 1-8 University of Ilorin

_____"The Use of Psalms in African Indigenous Churches in Nigeria," West, Gerald, Dube, Musa. Editors. *The Bible in Africa: Transactions, Trajectories and Trends*. Boston: Brill. 2000, 336-349.

Adeboyejo, T. N. *Saint Michael Prayer Book* (Lagos: Neye Ade & Sons, 1988), 21.

Ademiluka, Olusola. "The Use of Psalms in African Context," M.A Thesis, University of Ilorin, 1991

Adewole, S.A. *The Revelation of God for 1992 and the Years Ahead* (Lagos: Sam Adewole, 1991), 22.

_____*Awake Celetians, Satan is Nearer* (Lagos; Celetia Church of Christ, Opopo-Igbala, Ikola Rd, 1991) 45-45.

Agoro, Roland. *Sixteen Names of God* (Ibadan:Olapade Agoro Investment Co.Ltd, 1984.

Awolalu, J.O.*Biblical Revelation and African Beliefs* (eds) K. Dickson and P. Ellingsworth. New York: Orbis.Books, 1969

Barret, Davd . *Schism and Renewal in Africa* (Oxford University Press, 1968), 166.

Bolarinwa, J.A. *Potency and Efficacy of Psalms*(Ibadan: Oluseyi Press, n.d), 8.

Brown, Raymond. *An Introduction to the New Testament*. New York: Doubleday, 1997.

Gordon Clinard. "Biblical Preaching on Suffering," *Southwestern Journal of Theology*. (April 1963), 33-41.

_____"Biblical Preaching on Suffering," *Southwestern Journal of Theology* (SWJTH), April 1959, 20

Cone, James. *A Black Theology of Liberation.* Philadelphia: Lippincott, 1970

Cone, J. and Wilmore, G. eds., *Black Theology: A Documentary History, 1966-1979* (Maryknoll, N.Y: Orbis Books, 1979.

Dopamu, P.A. *Esu: The Invisible Foe of Man.* Ijebu-Ode: Shebiotimo Publications, 1986), 57.

_____ " The Reality of Isaasi, Apeta, Ironsi and Efun as forces of Evil among the Yoruba," *Journal Arabic and Religious Studies* 4 Dec. 1987):50-61;

_____ "Epe: The Magic of Curse among the Yoruba," *Religions* 8 (Dec.1983), 1-11.

Dryness, W. *Themes in Old Testament Theology* .Downer Grove: Inter-varsity Press, 1979

Eichrodt, W. *Theology of the Old Testament.* Philadelphia: The Westmister Press, 1961. Vol. 1.

Felder, Cain Hope. *Stony the Road We Trod.* (Ed.) Minneapolis: Fortress Press, 1991)

Foerster, W.editor G. Kittel, *Theological Dictionary of the New Testament*, Vol. II Translated by Geoffrey W. Bromiley, Grand Rapids: WM B. Eerdmans Publishing Company, 1982

Holter, Knut. *Yahweh in Africa. Essays on Africa and the Old Testament.* New York: Peter Lang Publishing, Inc. 2000

Mulrain, G. "Hermeneutics within a Caribean Context," *Vernacular Hermeneutics*, ed. R.S Sugirtharajah (Sheffeild: Sheffied Academy Press, 1999

Harris,R.L, Archer,L Jr and Waltke, B.K 'Shalom', *Theological Wordbook of the Old Testament* (Chicago: Moody Bible Institute, 1981), 2401.

Colin Brown, General Editor, 'Peace', *The New International Dictionary of the New Testament*.Grand Rapids; Zondervan Publishing House, 1982

Idowu, E.B, *Olodumare God in Yoruba Belief* London: Longmans, 1962

James, Weldon Johnson. ed. *The Book of American Negro Spirituals* New York:Viking Press, 1925

Maultsby, P.K. "Africanism in African-American Music," in *Africanism in American Culture*, Joseph E. Holloway (ed) (Bloomington, Indiana: Indiana University Press, 1990), 185-210.

Mitchell, H. *Black Preaching: The Recovery of a Powerful Art* (Nashville: Abingdon Press, 1990)

Mbiti, J.S. *Concepts of God in Africa* London: S.P.C.K., 1970

Mume, J.O. *Traditional Medicine in Nigeria* (Agbarho: Jom Tradomedical Naturopathic Hospital ,1978)

Ogunfuye, J. *The Secrets of the Uses of Psalms* (Ibadan: Ogunfuye Publication, n.d)

Robinson, W. *Suffering Human and Divine* .New York: The Macmillan Comp. 1939), 3.

Sanders, Jim. "Suffering as Divine Discipline in the Old Testament and Post Biblical Judiasm," *Colgate Rochester Divinity School Bulletin*, (1955)42.

Sugirtharajah, R.S. "Vernacular Resurrections: An Introduction," *Vernacular Hermeneutics*, (ed.). Sheffield: Sheffield Academic Press, 1999.

Ubrurhe, J. " Life and Healing Processes in Urhobo Medicine," *Humanitas* (1994) vol. 1, New Series, forth coming.

Ukpong, J.S. "Can African Old Testament Scholarship escape the historical critical approach?" *Newsletter on African Old Testament Scholarship*, Knut Holter (ed.), no 7, (1999),

_____ " Reading the Bible with African Eyes," *Journal of Theology for Southern Africa (JTSA)*, (June 1995),3-14.

Weiser, A. *The Psalms, Old Testament Library*, trans. By Herbert Hartwell Philadelphia: The Westmister Press, 1962

_____*Out of Depths: the Psalms Speak for us Today* (Philadelphia: The Westminster Press, 1974)

Westermann, Claus. *Praise and Lament in the Psalms*, translated by K.R Crim and Richard N Soulen (Atlanta: John Knox Press, 1981), 52,64.

Yorke, G.L, "Biblical Hermeneutics:an Afrocentric Perspective,"*Journal of Religion and Theology*, vol 2, no 2(1995), 145-158

www.ingramcontent.com/pod-product-compliance
Lightning Source LLC
Chambersburg PA
CBHW051937160426
43198CB00013B/2190